ATROPOS PRESS
new york • dresden

ATROPOS PRESS
New York - Dresden
151 First Avenue # 14, New York, N.Y. 10003

Cover image and design: Anne-Laure Oberson

ISBN 978-0-9885170-11

I see. do you?
Thinking seeing.

Anne-Laure Oberson

Acknowledgements

I am grateful, first and foremost, to my husband for encouraging me to step on the philosophical path and for his unfailing support along the way; to our daughter for her joy.

I would like to offer my warmest thanks to Wolfgang Schirmacher for his inspiring rage and his commitment to education; to Joshua Hammerling for his proofreading and comments; to Jamie Allen for his close reading of the final text, the many precious corrections and enlightening suggestions; to all my teachers at the European Graduate School and fellow students for their generosity in sharing their knowledge, and especially to Thomas Zummer for pointing the direction.

TABLE OF CONTENT

"…our point of view, once valid in its singularity, has been broken up into an infinite diversity of perspectives. The unexpected constellations of these perspectives, their chance interplay which gives rise to temporary ideas and images, require a new art of perception." [1]

W. Schirmacher

[1] Wolfgang Schirmacher, "Art(ificial) Perception: Nietzsche and Culture After Nihilism," *Poesis* (1999): 4.

Introduction

"The act of photography is one of phenomenological doubt."[1] I see, in common parlance, means I understand. It is by seeing the world around us that we can begin to understand it (Plato). This implies that since man can see, man can think. Thus, and in as much as philosophy is a phenomenological endeavour, the evolution of vision and its study has been tightly entangled with the development of philosophy since its inception. Any new addition to the apparatuses of vision – the mirror, spectacles, telescope, radiography, microscope, camera obscura, etc. – has had deep repercussions for our modes of perception and consequently on our modes of philosophizing.
Of all inventions, photography not only mediates human vision like preceding instruments, but also fixes it; by introducing duration to a continuous faculty, it reinforces the possibilities of vision in a phenomenological act as it makes it last and gives us the time to reflect upon it.

So, if photography is not the phenomenological assertion that it has been understood as since its invention, but is now being reconsidered by the visionary thinker Vilém Flusser as casting a doubt rather than being a proof, then certainly a new look at the relation between photography, image making, viewing, perceiving through vision has to be considered.

---

[1] Vilém Flusser, *Towards a Philosophy of Photography* (London: Reaktion, 2000), 38.

To what degree is how we think determined by how we see? And what we think by what we see? How do we see? And is our ability to think determined by our ability to see? What do we mean exactly when we say "I see." And what do we see exactly?

Thinking is primarily – solely, most would claim – framed by language, but it is also in good part due to our ability to project mental images – concepts – into a flow of consciousness. Wolfgang Schirmacher underlines the complexities of this subject and opens the door to look beyond words: "There is communication beyond written or spoken language which is as powerful as it is silent. And it can be increasingly observed that in communication a language based on words is a part, and not the whole. Pictures and sounds, silence and performances, an art-filled space and body language speak their own mind."[1]

Much has been written about the formation of thoughts and language from the perspective of phenomenology, visual perception, neurophysiology, psychology, and to account for these writings is beyond the scope of this present essay. Few aspects of the recent developments in these fields since the advent of digital photography will be addressed only as they are relevant to the advancing argument.

[1] Wolfgang Schirmacher, "Media Aesthetics in Europe," presented at the The Media in Europe, Paris: Association Descartes and College International de Philosophie, 1991, http://www.egs.edu/faculty/wolfgang-schirmacher/articles/media-aesthetics-in-europe/.

In March 2011, walking down the street where I live on the way to work one early Tuesday morning, after I had watched online events then taking place in Tunisia, Egypt and Libya, the cover of an original LP album displayed in the front window of the Pan African Cultural Center caught my eye: a reclining young black man, dressed in earth tone cool wool against a yellow background, the words in the upper right corner which read THE REVOLUTION / WILL NOT BE / TELEVISED / GIL SCOTT-HERON. It spurred me into thinking. The hit song came out in the 60s. Indeed 50 years later the revolution remains untelevised, just as Scott-Heron predicted. It is TELE-vised in a Virilian rather than a McLuhan way.
A propos these recent revolutions, and pertaining to the questions just raised, images reached us long before any text had even the time to be written: instantaneously they appeared on our mobile devices, thus conditioning solely through vision our perception of events that would be contextualized, commented, explained, justified through language only afterwards.

The departure point of this thesis is the seminal text by Vilém Flusser *Towards a Philosophy of Photography*, first published in German in 1983. This concise philosophical essay raises key questions regarding the logic of representation, revisits completely the traditional understanding of photography, turns the medium inside out and forces us to stop taking prior critical milestones for granted.

In light of Flusser's hypothesis, the present essay will investigate how a single image holds all other images. I argue that photography is neither a fixed medium, nor does it fix anything; rather, it is transient, fluid, undetermined, floating. It does not respond to the Barthian logic of "ça a été" (it has been) but to a constantly renewed "c'est" (it is), which is always in becoming. Hence photography is never a witness.

The following pages will present different historical modes of thinking the image and explore what it means today as a carrier of information. The image is no longer distinctly where images happen: whether in our mind, in the form of mental images, or out there, in front of our eyes, there is no longer a dialectical logic of the in and out, but the presence of one permeable torrent/fabric/mass, a volumatic field of correspondences. I call it *fasciae* in reference to the connective tissue, composed of evening news, memories, snapshot, synthetic images, dreams, fantasies, artworks, etc. that belong to the collective memory, that respond to a quantum logic, and that impact how we conceive of the thinking process.

Additionally, the shift from the materiality to the immateriality of the photograph, from paper-based to electricity-based images, has completely changed the way the visual information is presented to us and how we process it, relate to it, and how these images form our consciousness, our thoughts and are shared.

On this last point, particular emphasis is placed on the quantum quality of photographic images.

Throughout the text, the word "image" is used in its broadest meaning. In writing of images, reference is made to 2D visual representations that are analogical or digital, technical or synthetic, original or reproduced, found or created, of any dimension and quality, on any support – including the brain. I strictly write of still images and understand most images to be of photographic nature, since today even paintings are most of the time encountered in their mechanical reproduction. These images have primarily and increasingly been produced these past 20 years.

Looking Back

Objects in mirror are closer than they appear

The critical history of photography has been written predominantly by art historians and literary critics, which are communities interested in links to "the real", hence the discourse is heavily set around the question of the index, thus making reference to the past and metaphorically to death. Since the time of its creation photography has been conceived and presented as a representation of the real, an imprint of the object that lies in front of the camera, an index inseparable from its referent, an objective witness. Today's images are bodiless and ubiquitous, they form a surrounding field, not something linear, not circular, not even only rhizomatic any longer, but something of the order of the sphere, a volume in the middle of which the seer is located. This field formed by millions of photographs demands that photography is given new consideration. It calls for new definitions, new ideas, new words, new texts. The most provocative to date is a text written by Vilém Flusser, whose brilliant thinking opens a way ahead:

> [...] the traditional distinction between realism and idealism is overturned in the case of photography: It is not the world out there that is real, nor is the concept within the camera's program – only the photograph is real. [...] It is not the significance that is real but the signifier, the information, the symbol, and this reversal of the vector of significance is characteristic

> of everything to do with apparatus and characteristic of the post-industrial world in general.[1]

With these claims Vilém Flusser ousts 150 years of conceptualizating photography. In an equally incisive manner, Geoffrey Batchen ruptures endless litanies about photography's indexicality by using the exact same semiological source on which these are based. Batchen, with reference to Peirce and Derrida, blows away the threat posed to it by its digital variation: "Real and representation must, according to Peirce's own argument, always already inhabit each other. As Derrida points out, in Peirce's writing 'the thing in itself' is a sign... from the moment there is meaning there are nothing but signs."[2]

These original thinkers pave the way for a complete re-conceptualization of photography, and much work still needs to be done to unbolt traditional ideas firmly established by early historians and critics, and regenerated by their postmodern counterparts.

TEXTUAL BACKGROUND

Indeed, if one looks at the bibliographical sources of those who have written on photography up to the early nineties, the evidence shows how few and how similar the references are; most belong to the domain of

---

[1] Flusser, *Towards a Philosophy of Photography*, 37.

[2] Geoffrey Batchen, "Ectoplasm: Photography in the Digital Age," in *Over Exposed* (New York: New Press, 1999), 21.

literary criticism, art history or critical theory; a few refer to psychoanalysis, via the Surrealists; but none reach outside these philological academic fields into science or technology. This is disquieting considering that photography is a technology that has had a tremendous impact on vision and perception.[1] It is also surprising that very little philosophical consideration has been given to photography, even though so many philosophers write about vision, which is the phenomenological sense par excellence.

There are a few seminal texts written on photography that have shaped our understanding of the media almost once and for all. The two most influential ones are Walter Benjamin's *The Work of Art in the Age of Mechanical Reproduction*[2] in 1936 and Roland Barthes' *La chambre claire* in 1980; they are also most often quoted in critical discussions about photography.[3] In the 40 year lapse that separates those two essays, a handful of dedicated texts have been written, the most consequential being Szarkowski's *The Photographer's Eye* in 1966 and Berger's *Ways of Seeing* in 1972 (published after the popular BBC TV series). In their time, these texts were to some extent visionary, but they are

[1] Perhaps this has been so in order to keep inscribing photography within the field of the arts that it had a hard time accessing in the first place.

[2] It is under this translated title that it was published in the book *Illuminations* (1968, 1984), a selection of his essays by Hanah Arendt. Only later the translation was corrected to "The work of art in the age of its technological reproductibility" to match faithfully the original german title.

[3] This is obvious in perusing James Elkins, *Photography Theory* (New York: Routledge, 2007).

no longer valid in regard to the extended nature of photography today. There would be further research to be done for writing on photography outside of western institutions and discourse, that may enlighten us beyond the premonitory and now famous remark by the Hungarian artist Laszlo Moholy-Nagy: "The illiterate of the future will be ignorant of the use of camera and pen alike."[1]

With the 1980s, art historians Rosalind Krauss, Benjamin Buchloh, Douglas Crimp took on the discussion of photography within postmodern artistic practices. These critics formed a discourse that frequently dipped into psychology, but that disregarded other significant fields of study such as neurobiology or philosophy.
There are other singular figures, such as Allan Sekula, Alan Trachtenberg, Victor Burgin, Abigail Solomon Godeau, whose texts have influenced photographers and are of great importance within the field of practice, but which are not cited by the academics and therefore have had less impact on the discourse. John Berger's TV series and Victor Burgin's collection of essays have reached a large audience principally in the UK, if we take the number of reprints as any indication. More recently the curator Carol Squiers has published interesting collections on photography that group the independent voices of Timothy Drucrey and Geoffrey Batchen amongst others; Hubertus von Amelunxen and his timely 1995 exhibition *Photography after Photography*,

[1] Laszlo Moholy Nagy, "From Pigment to Light (1936)," in *Photography in Print* (Albuquerque: University of New Mexico Press, 1988), 348.

the catalogue from which addresses contemporary issues that venture outside the field.

Perhaps the lack of critical interest for photography is in part due to the emergence of "new media" and the fields of cultural studies and visual culture studies, which have attracted a great deal of the attention since the mid-sixties and seventies. The resurgence of interest in the eighties corresponds to an intentional postmodern use of photography by artists. This late appropiation of photography by the field of "high" contemporary art brought it to attention in a sudden manner, when we remember the struggle photography has had to be seriously considered within the Fine Arts since its invention.

Truly original attempts to think photography in and of itself remain marginal. Flusser, Van Lier, and to some extent Manovich have all tried to rethink the contemporary image. These thinkers open the door to some radical new thinking and demand of us a plurality of approaches that is duly needed, since prior conceptions do not reflect the complexities of contemporary (digital) photography nor consider the radical scientific developments around perception and memory.
The understanding of photography has been constructed on a handful of concepts, which have now become popular clichés endowed with an enduring capacity to stick around: indexicality (imprint), reality, death, window, etc. – and therefore they must be challenged and dealt with. The medium of photography is still in its

infancy even though some already speak in term of post-photography or have proclaimed or are anxious about its death.[1] As a toddler, photography will go through a few further developmental phases, acquire new skills, err, and is unlikely to die soon.

From the perspective of the practicing photographer, as well as the art historian, and with the ambition to engage in philosophical considerations, this essay serves a speculative place of encounter for these various points of view.

THE SHIFT FROM ANALOGUE TO DIGITAL

"Digital technology does not subvert 'normal' photography because 'normal' photography never existed."[2] It actually contributes to making photography even more familiar. The digital revolution has blurred the overall picture and fogged the clarity of the discourse around the technical production and status of images, creating a good deal of uncertainty and a lot of fundamental and ethical questioning on the nature of the act of photography. Now with the distance of roughly 30 years of practice and writings, we are starting to have enough material and references to begin looking back and reflecting.

---

[1] In this essay, photography is understood as a medium in the sense of a method and an apparatus of production, and not as a media, an agency or means of communicating or diffusing information.

[2] Lev Manovich, "The Paradoxes of Digital Photography," in *Photography After Photography* (Munich: Praterinsel, 1996).

As Lev Manovich very clearly explains it in his foresighted text of 1995 *The Paradoxes of Digital Photography,* photography is a medium that underwent radical changes in the course of its relatively brief history, to the extent that a single appellation refers to completely different processes from the first experiments to the latest fiber-optic captures.

> The logic of the digital photograph is one of historical continuity and discontinuity. The digital image tears apart the net of semiotic codes, modes of display, and patterns of spectatorship in modern visual culture -- and, at the same time, weaves this net even stronger. The digital image annihilates photography while solidifying, glorifying and immortalizing the photographic. In short, this logic is that of photography after photography.[1]

It is important to signal here that Manovich mentions a photography after the photography we think we know, and does not use the concept of "post-photography" that David Tomas strongly establishes in his essay and which becomes problematic together with his claim of the end of history. Although it is to be conceded that "images will now float fragmented, incoherent, but free in a perceptual present, the continuous product of contextual oscillations between the unhistorical and the historical"[2], what happens is mostly a relocation of the eye rather than a disappearance and what is needed more than ever before is a point of view. The concept

---

[1] Ibid.

[2] David Tomas, "From the Photograph to Postphotographic Practice: Toward a Postoptical Ecology of the Eye," *Substance* no. 55 (1988): 66.

of history is certainly going under radical changes, but its disappearance would entail the disappearance of the written word.

The claim of the difference between analogue and digital photography is no longer a valid argument in terms of perception and in defining the status of the image (except perhaps for fetishist reasons or market values) as the former is now completely merged into the latter: all museums have digitized their collections (the Hermitage Museum started in 1996, MoMA in 1997) for conservation reasons as well as practical access to images and their diffusion; all industrial processing labs scan conventional film strips in order to produce prints. This is so to such an extent, that most of our access to analogue images (including paintings and drawings) is mediated through a digital stage, phase or production process, whether we are looking at websites, TV screens or even books.

From this perspective, the very discussion about the continuous versus the discreet nature of the photograph has been irrelevant since the use of offset printing and the halftone screen, which already then had broken the continuous image in discreet overlapping dots playing optically to render a smooth continuous perceptual surface. Not to mention that the concept of continuity is not even pertinent when we talk about visual perception since we have known for some time that saccadic eye movements are necessary in the illusion of a continuous vision and more recent neurological studies show that natural visual stimuli provoke brief firing neural responses.[1]

The digital shift, which has frightened many and which some have claimed would be the death of photography, happens not to be so great. Digital imagery is at once very different, yet strangely the same.

> The digitisation of photography simply means its translation into a numerically coded – and therefore non-visual – legibility, a translation which it shares with the other media of sound, writing or film. [...] Thus digitisation offers us new kinds of image spaces in which the possibilities of modulation are limited by arithmetic alone and in which the links with reality can be shifted arbitrarily. Image and space, representation, the historical archive and the human archive (memory with its elementary contiguity) are destined to be subjected to an as yet inconceivable revision.[2]

Yet photography has always been a coded medium. Indeed, as Flusser explains at length in his attempt at a philosophy of photography, the photograph has always been the result of a program – "a combination game with clear and distinct elements" (symbols).[3] Technical images respond to "a universally valid code", they are "the lowest common denominator for art, science and

---

[1] It is in 1878 that Louis Emile Javes wrote about saccades to describe the movements done by the eyes during reading. For further reading on visual neurons refer to Pamela Reinagel's article "How Do visual Neurons Respond in the Real World?," 2001, http://www.ncbi.nlm.nih.gov/pubmed/11502389.

[2] Hubertus von Amelunxen, "The Terror of the Body in Digital Space," in *Photography After Photography* (Munich: Praterinsel, 1995).

[3] Flusser, *Towards a Philosophy of Photography*, 84.

politics."[1] So the shift is in the location of the arithmetic: if the program resides only in a "black box" the output of which is analogous to the world "out there", now the output of the digital camera program remains a program. It remains so as images more and more often do not end up in printed form but remain encoded on the screen. Hence the shift is not were it is expected, in the symbolic value, the reference, but in the very form and content of the medium. Images have become texts.

There has always been a mediating agent, or a "vehicle" to use a term favored by Paul Virilio. This passage of photography from analogue to digital marks a second paradigm shift in the historical construction of vision. The first one, described as such by Jonathan Crary in his essay *Techniques of the Observer,* published in *October* in 1988, is the emergence in the nineteenth century of the spectator as a figure with the birth of a new type of vision made possible by the embodiment of the eyes. At some point in the course of the twentieth century, the very same spectator lost touch with this first-hand apprehension of the image: television – says it in all letters. This tele-vision is the first step in the disembodiment of the image. In his book *The Vision Machine,* Virilio roots this process in the invention of the telescope and the concurrent disembodiment of our vision from a physical experience to a mental exercise.
The mass appearance and adoption of screens originates with the cinema and later with the cathode ray

---

[1] Ibid., 19.

tube (CRT) but its domination is proportional to that of the personal computer (PC) and increased rapidly with its portability and applicability. It is the mobility of computing that has allowed screens to become omnipresent. With the cinema and television, a relation to the screen is still totally codependent on space and time. With analogue photography, so is the production of content, it is only its diffusion that is disconnected. "Photography *was* understood in its relationship to the co-ordinates of space and time in which it originated and which left their mark on it."[1]

Henceforth all such relations burst into pieces. With the digital, the net and the wireless, there is no longer any correlation whatsoever between these dimensions of the image. There is even a multiplication of spaces and times, a coalescence rendered possible by the simultaneous presence of several independent screens in the same location at the same time but each connected to very different spaces and times.
Is it ubiquity or is it the exact opposite, since the seer is not in many places at once but the many places are present at the site of the seer? The disconnection of space and time is double as it happens at the level of the spectator (diffusion) and at the level of the image (production) which is itself no longer dependent on the correlation of these parameters:

> Analogo-numerical photography imposes a new grammatical direction on our seeing. Our habitualised power of visual

---

[1] Amelunxen von, "The Terror of the Body in Digital Space." My emphasis.

> perception is destined to be directly effected not only by the manipulation of the image, which cannot be traced back to a material origin, but above all by the general availability of images as sets of data capable of being managed and interchanged endlessly. Even if the analogo-numerical image can still be recognised via its representative values, the photographic image will no longer be able to qualify as a translation of a spatio-temporal moment. The analogo-numerical image is separated from its origin, its negative. It is without a shadow. Seeing is impeded in its elementary process of recognition and is unable to achieve a translation of what it recognises into memory, which is grounded in representation.[1]

This freedom from these coordinates allows for an unprecedented acceleration of the diffusion of images.

Last, the new model of vision rendered possible by digital imaging is actually closer to human vision than analogue imaging ever was as it delocalises vision from the eye to the brain as we will elaborate in the next section.

THE QUESTION OF THE REAL

> For what is faked is, of course, not reality but photographic reality, reality as seen by the camera lens. In other words, what computer graphics has (almost) achieved is not realism, but only photorealism – the ability to fake not our perceptual and bodily experience of reality but only its photographic image. This image exists outside of our consciousness, on a screen – a

[1] Ibid.

> window of limited size which presents a still imprint of a small part of outer reality, filtered through the lens with its limited depth of field, filtered through film's grain and its limited tonal range. It is only this film-based image which computer graphics technology has learned to simulate. And the reason we think that computer graphics has succeeded in faking reality is that we, over the course of the last hundred and fifty years, have come to accept the image of photography and film as reality.[1]

The question of the existence of a real is a precarious one. It is in physics, as it is in philosophy. Many have tackled it from all angles and many disagree strongly as it resists as firmly as the question of consciousness. When it comes to the field of photography, it is particularly enduring, since the toughest conditional prerequisite of photography is the representation of the real. Whatever the real might be, photography has always been concerned with it, inasmuch as it has allowed depicting the invisible, the unseable and even giving appearance to the supranatural.

What is paradoxical in the relation of photography with reality is that, as much as it pretends to assert it and verify it via its representation, it contributes in great parts to its demise. Before photography there was likely much less doubting the everyday; when the jar of milk stopped being merely on the table, but was also simultaneously framed on the wall and set in an album laying in the drawer, then problems began...
Photography has always been too real for its own good.

---

[1] Manovich, "The Paradoxes of Digital Photography."

From hyper real to less than real, the photograph changes our perception of what we accept or learn to see, if not neurobiologically at least intellectually and emotionally. In the essay *On Realism in Art* Roman Jakobson makes a very convincing demonstration:

> The methods of projecting three-dimensional space onto a flat surface are established by convention; the use of color, the abstracting, the simplification, of the object depicted, and the choice of reproducible features are all based on convention. It is necessary to learn the conventional language of painting in order to 'see' a picture, just as it is impossible to understand what is spoken without knowing the language. This conventional, traditional aspect of painting to a great extent conditions the very act of our visual perception. As tradition accumulates, the painted image becomes an ideogram, a formula, to which the object portrayed is linked by contiguity. Recognition becomes instantaneous. We no longer see a picture.[1]

This passage is cited in William J. Mitchell's *The Reconfigured Eye* in order to verify the reality effect of certain images, but instead what Jakobson reveals here is the mechanism of illusion. The eye has been trained to read a picture like real images in the same manner it has learned to know that a painting is not reality. And the eye then comes to recognise the world as an image. What we see and can comprehend is only a construction of the brain. And most often a construction that responds to and follows acquired cultural conventions. The question of context is hence primordial.

---

[1] William J. Mitchell, *The Reconfigured Eye. Visual Truth in the Post-photographic Era*, 3rd ed. (Cambridge, MA: MIT Press, 1998), 27.

But today the ubiquity of an image at any phase of its existence, whether during its production, its diffusion or while it is stored, means a lesser control over a singular context in exchange for great variability of contexts for any given image; thus interpretations of images are likely to differ enormously. "In forming interpretations of images, then, we use evidence of the parts to suggest possible interpretations of the whole, and we use the context of the whole to suggest possible interpretations of the parts."[1]

The images [video stills] of the first Iraq war bombings at night over Bagdad resemble stills from a video game. There is something utterly banal, a sense of déjà-vu; the synthetic low quality that established the distance allowed for this trivializing of views that should be truly shocking.

> There was no Mathew Brady to show us the bodies on the ground, no Robert Capa to confront us with the human reality of a bullet through the head. Instead, the folks back home were fed carefully selected, electronically captured, sometimes digitally processed images of distant and impersonal destruction. Slaughter became a video game: death imitated art.[2]

This creates a sense of confusion, which is an unsurprising reaction when the referent is lost. Images of the destruction of the Twin Towers echoed in our mind with images from the movie *The Towering Inferno* (1974)

---

[1] Ibid., 34.

[2] Ibid., 13.

and thus something in our cognitive reaction is set off: these *déjà-views* are not of the order of a neurological glitch, but pertain to our accessing a collective memory that is reactivated. We have seen it all.

We stand between shock and awe because up until our current era these images that we have learned to take for reality are fiction, there is a coalescence of one regime onto the other, a crashing of distances. This is really startling because there is no more space for fantasy or banality; there is a play on familiarity, there is no longer anything uncanny. There is no surprise only discomfort: what is unsettling is not the content (as it should be) but the fact that the image has already been in front of our eyes before. We are thus left once again with the question: What do we see?

Eye to brain

There have been many extraordinary ways in which man has tried to explain the fascinating sense of vision, from the Atomists' understanding that a substance, "a material effluence" had to come in "direct contact with the organ of sense"[1], to the Platonic theory of a visual current coming from the eye, a "visual fire emanates from the eye and coalesces with its like, daylight, to form 'a single homogeneous body' stretching from the

[1] David C. Lindberg, *Theories of Vision from Al-Kindi to Kepler* (Chicago & London: University of Chicago Press, 1981), 2.

eye to the visible object" [1], from which an emanation also occurs, to Aristotle's conception of a medium, the transparent, air, through which we see. From Euclid we get a strictly mathematical account of vision, an explaination in details of its geometry. Ptolemy's most comprehensive and extended theory encompasses his predecessors' analyses and refines them: he defines the conical shape of the visual flux from the eye and locates the position of its apex. Not until Alhazen was there a work which fused anatomical, physical and mathematical explanations into one comprehensive theory of vision, whose conceptions were at the source of Kepler's modern theory. [2] By each of these accounts, vision is far from a purely mechanical activity.
After being embodied by the new sciences of the 19th century, the eye is again disembodied as it is merely a channel for the information that is processed and constructed into an image not on the retina but deep within the brain.

The history of the theories of vision is complex, challenging and spans across disciplines.
The art historian Jonathan Crary identified a shift in the 19th century with the advent of photography and new biological sciences, which can be inversely replicated in the 20th century in terms not of embodiment but of a distancing, dematerialisation and a reconceptualization of vision. The apparatus doesn't stand in for

---

[1] Ibid., 5.

[2] Ibid., 86.

the eye anymore but for the whole body. The experience is reversed from individual to collective, from private back to public. This is marked by the passage from the camera-lens to the camera-screen.

> The primary sense organ of photography is a mobile camera/eye, which echoes the structure and instrumental functions of the human biological eye. Its lens, however, is made of glass, its retina is a photosensitive surface and its 'optic nerve' is a perceiving authorial consciousness. In contrast to this all-seeing cultural artifact; the postphotographic 'eye' has no need of a lens and its darkened chamber, the mediums for the differentiation, focusing and fixation of point of view. Postphotography is no longer modeled on an optical consciousness operating independently of its material and symbolic contexts. Its mirror-like surfaces, which correspond to 'raw' retinas, provide pretexts to continuously contextualize and metacontextualize systemic visual processes of production.[1]

With the appearance of the screen, the image maker does not look attentively with one eye in the viewfinder but skims the backlit screen of his capturing device (one can no longer restrictively speak of a camera, since phones, tablets and watches also function as image capturing tools) held at a distance from his body. Such a shift in viewpoint and body-apparatus relation had already happened when the small format camera freed photographers from their belly-button point of view. Paradoxically, at the same time as the process of image making becomes more and more individual

[1] Tomas, "From the Photograph to Postphotographic Practice: Toward a Postoptical Ecology of the Eye," 65–66.

and privatized, to the point of rendering developing and printing labs obsolete, the distribution of images become increasingly public, as the most insignificant and personal snaps are being shared with the world at large on the internet. Schirmacher further emphasises this paradox when he states: "Instead of media for the masses we can observe the birth of a potential media of the masses. Only with regard to distribution is mass still a topic, in terms of audience we are back to tailor-made programming and inventions."[1]

These paradoxical and almost antagonistic developments, which are happening at once, radically change the interactions and relations with and to the image. With these, the nature of the image has changed in accord. Indeed we are also viewing images of a completely different type:

> So rather than being an aberration, a flaw in the otherwise pure and perfect world of the digital, where even a single bit of information is never lost, lossy compression is increasingly becoming the very foundation of digital visual culture. This is another paradox of digital imaging: while in theory digital technology entails the flawless replication of data, its actual use in contemporary society is characterized by the loss of data, degradation, and noise; the noise which is even stronger than that of traditional photography.[2]

Therefore, the concern is how do these degradations in representation contribute to the degradation in our

[1] Schirmacher, "Media Aesthetics in Europe."

[2] Manovich, "The Paradoxes of Digital Photography."

ways of looking, both in the high end of HD TV which reveals too many details and turns 'unreal' compared to the relative inaccuracy of unmediated human vision and in the low range of pixelated, flat video stills that we are growing increasingly used to?

COGNITIVE CONSTRUCTION

If man is a creature of habit, conditional reflexes, biological determination, how is it that his perception happens to change? As some of the aforementioned writers have demonstrated, it is often due to a conjunction of different factors such as techniques, discoveries, knowledge, instruments that are gradually changing the modes, thus the senses of perception.

In contemporary times, these transformations happen ever more frequently and rapidly. For example, let's think how quickly one learns new gestures necessary to operate a latest technical device – swiping one's fingers across a screen is a quite radically recent gesture, one that only a couple of years ago was not common practice. Of course such gestures exist in potential; this particular one previously linked to a specific function: the turning of a page in a book. But with this new attribution and in its subtleties, it is fair to say that it is a new gesture, a new interaction with images. Let us witness how fingers move above the keyboard when the user switches between the Microsoft Windows or the Apple Mac platforms – even though the user knows both sets of commands and is fully aware of which platform s/he is currently using, the gesture will precisely, by default, direct itself to the combination that is most familiar. How unnerving, after having recently moved house, when we inadvertentily take the wrong route to an old home address. Examples are countless, some skills take years to master, some minutes to acquire, but a change in the simplest habit takes conscious effort.

These concerns are mainly physical (motor coordination) but they apply equally to other senses: the ringer of a new cell phone doesn't call one's attention for a few days but the ringtone of one's first cell phone will still result in a grasping for it years after it's been discarded.
So now let's imagine something that is more difficult to grasp: how the same mechanisms might apply to what we see. If you just bought a red car, you will then see red cars where before you saw none; if she is pregnant, she will see babies all around her. It is not that the count of red cars and babies has suddenly risen but that the attention, the concern of one's gaze has come into renewed focus.

These examples show explicitly how what we see is not solely an exercice of visual perception but how closely it is linked to awareness. How have, or how will, our capacities for vision change with new technologies and new habits? Isn't looking at the screen at a distance of a mere 30cm gradually teaching us to lose our farsightedness?

In terms of neurological processes, an Italian study has shown that looking at a cut in the flesh (a wound), a Caravaggio painting of St. Tomas digging his finger in Christ's cut flank or a Fontana painting from the cut series provokes the same identical neurological responses.[1] As far as the interpretations of MRI scans report, brain activity is similar whether we look at a live performance or at the same performance displayed on a screen.

But neuroimagery does not reveal all, it merely fragments an aesthetic experience into factors that can be analysed independently, and does not study together the visual impact with the emotional, motor and environmental contexts. It is thus demonstrated that emotionally and physically, seeing is not a straightforward activity. The eye is a trainable organ linked to a plastic brain. Seeing is inborn but looking is learned. Most people do not see, because they do not look. So again, what do we mean, when we say: "I see."?

"How we perceive our world is shaped by the media in such a fundamental way that perception and media become interchangeable."[2]

Many parameters contribute to the construction of an image in our head. It starts 'simply' by opening one's eyes and looking, but the image flux that ensues is not only transient, it is also stored and thus contributes to an archive of images, a sort of reference library

[1] A study presented by Chiara Cappelletto, professor at the Università degli Studi di Milano, in her talk on neuroesthetic at the Laboratoire des Neuro/Sciences humaines, Hôpitaux universitaires de Genève, 18.11.2011.

[2] Schirmacher, "Media Aesthetics in Europe."

to which our brain has a constant access, against which it can verify, test and refresh new information. Thomas Zummer would say: "It is always a citation."
This accumulation of data also contributes to our purely mental images, which are not the fruit of a direct looking at something, but are formed inside our brain, for example during dreams or even during daily conceptual activity. For some people, musicians for example, sounds project images, and of course to most of us, words do too.
All these complex intertwined sources of visual material are irremediably linked to a visual mode and contemplative tone, which set a context for their cognitive construction. Based on Brian Massumi's theories, if we take the entire visual field as raw data fed through our eyes to our brain, the question of focus is directly dependent on the affective tone.[1]
Additionnally, we also perceive with our motor system, so that the visual experience is always linked to our body movements.
On a very basic level, the question of focus is explained by the now famous and often cited study of Jakob von Uexküll and his differentiation between the *Umwelt*, the *Merkwelt* and the *Wirkwelt*, according to which the world is perceived in a particular subjective manner only so far as it falls within the necessity of an action.[2]

---

[1] Brian Massumi, *Parables for the Virtual: Movement, Affect, Sensation*, Post-Contemporary Interventions (Durham & London: Duke University Press Books, 2002).
[2] Jakob von Uexküll, *A foray into the worlds of animals and humans: with a theory of meaning*, trans. Joseph D. O'Neil (Minneapolis: University of Minnesota Press, 2010).

In other words the function is the essence of the object, and an object is recognized only if its function is known.

Once the object 'of interest' is perceived, its perception is also a question of interpretation: the brain constantly constructs a 3D model from 2D information, and in addition it builds color, as color doesn't exist per se, and maintains it constant: grass in the shade will still be 'perceived' as green eventhough it is in fact rather grey. "Vision is a complex perceptual and cognitive activity that builds at every instant a model that is biologically pertinent, coherent and faithful to the external reality."[1]

To further complicate the matter, our system of reasoning responds to a dual process theory.
The heuristic system is universal and independent of intelligence and memory. It is like intuition; it serves to construct an initial model that is later verified by additional models due to the analytical system, it is an unconscious process.
The analytical system is based on experience and acquired knowledge; it is slower and not necessarily better than the heuristic system in simple verifications although it is more reliable in complex problem solving.[2]

---

[1] Mario Raggenbass, *Le réel, c'est dans la tête*, Semaine international du Cerveau, Université de Genève, 10.03.2008, conference.
[2] Caroline Gauffroy and Pierre Barrouillet, "Heuristic and Analytic Processes in Mental Models for Conditional: An Integrative Developmental Theory.," *Developmental Review* no. 29 (2009): 249–282.

Vilém Flusser makes another dual distinction that serves as an interesting parallelism. At the basis of his philosophy, he breaks down information according to two ways of encoding the world:
Line (words) – which is a discourse of points, each point being a symbol of something out-there, a concept; and
Surface (images) – in place of the line to signify the world (for the masses) but for which we do not yet possess a logic to understand its structure as elaborate as the Aristotelian linear logic that we have for reading text.

Both line and surface are to be read but they are not decoded in the same way. Thus Flusser further explains how a text is read from left to right, top to bottom and offers the signification at the end; whereas an image is taken in its entirety, the signification is grasped immediately, then analysed according to paths offered in the structure of the image itself: there is a double reading, first synthetic (heuristic) then analytic that is particular to images. In images, the message is given first, and then it is taken apart; in the text, the parts compose the message that is given at the end.[1]

---

[1] Vilém Flusser, "Line and Surface (1973)," in *Writings*, 2. Aufl. (Minneapolis: University of Minnesota Press, 2005), 22.

This remark on the immediate character of the image is crucial to allow any further understanding of how any imaging device may perform. As Jonathan Crary demonstrates in several enlightening essays, a paradigmatic shift occurred over the last two decades of the 19th century thanks to clinical research in psychological and neurobiological fields, but also thanks to greater empirical knowledge leading to new theories in physics (wave theory of light) and physical optics as well as new techniques, that gave birth to "a fully embodied observer."[1] The main reason for this shift is the subjectivisation of vision, its autonomy and privatisation.

"Once the empirical truth of vision was determined to lie in the body, it was then that the senses and vision in particular were able to be annexed and controlled by external techniques of manipulation and stimulation." If vision lies in the body and is less dependent on nature, it can be controlled but it also provides one of "the conditions for the historical emergence of the notions of autonomous vision", which means that perceptual experience is now freed from a necessary relation to the exterior world.[2]

Vision, once the touchstone of empirical knowledge, was also becoming unreliable in the process: "The

[1] Jonathan Crary, "Unbinding Vision," *October* 68 (Spring 1994): 21.

[2] Ibid., 21–22.

subject, as a dynamic psychophysical organism, actively constructed the world around it through a layered complex of sensory and cognitive processes, of higher and lower cerebral centers."[1] Citing the works of Pierre Janet as one of the researchers who "discovered how volatile the perceptual field can be, and that dynamic oscillations of perceptual awareness and mild forms of dissociation were part of what was considered normative behavior."[2], Crary further demonstrates the indubitable subjective character of visual perception. And hence the need for new controlling and entertaining tools, until "the relation between the eye and optical apparatus becomes one of metonymy."[3]

The consequence of these new apparatuses, like the stereoscope for instance or even paradoxically the panorama, was the privatization of vision due to "an intensification of visuality and also an isolation of the subject from a lived embeddedness in a given social milieu"[4] that correspond to the "new isolated consumer of a mass-produced commodity"[5] as accounted for by Walter Benjamin in reference to the novel reader, or otherwise referred to by Crary as the modern spectator.

---

[1] Ibid., 33.

[2] Ibid., 33.

[3] Jonathan Crary, *Techniques of the Observer: on Vision and Modernity in the Nineteenth Century.* (Cambridge, MA: MIT Press, 1990), 31.

[4] Jonathan Crary, "Géricault, the Panorama, and Sites of Reality in the Early Nineteenth Century.," *Grey Room* no. 9 (Autumn 2002): 15.

[5] Ibid., 8.

There is a great paradox that resonates today about this privatisation of sight.
On one hand, the viewer is thus separated from his contextual environment and the image detaches itself from the background in both the peep-show and the panorama model, which "involves a detachment of the image from a wider field of possible sensory stimulation and creates a calculated confusion about the literal location of the painted surface as a way of enhancing its illusions of presence and distance."[1]
On the other hand, the large exhibition displays and other international fairs popular at the time, made the 19th century spectator of a painting "an observer who simultaneously encountered a proliferating diversity of optical and sensory experiences" as paintings were both produced and displayed "as one of the many consumable and fleeting elements within an expanding field of images, commodities, and attractions."[2]

Much to the contrary, in the 20th century, paintings are exalted behind museum doors and belong to a sacred register of images, becoming a source of great fetishism. But simultaneously there is a levelling of their status as images, since all the genres, forms, sizes and shapes of produced images end up on a singular format: the pixelated lossy image file readily available to all in the privacy of the glowing light of the personal screen.

---

[1] Ibid., 19.

[2] Ibid., 12–13.

One last parallel to be made between the 19th century panorama and the 21st century panoramic vision proposed by various viewing softwares: the panorama, as described by Crary, "posed a view of a motif [...] that seemed immediately accessible but that always exceeded the capacity of a spectator to grasp it [...], is consumable only as fragments, as parts that must be cognitively reassembled into an imagined whole [...], seems magically to overcome the fragmentation of experience [but] in fact introduces partiality and incompletedness as constitutive elements of visual experience."[1]
This description is exactly reversely applicable to the image banks of today, and to the way we encounter technical images within the digital landscape. Not only can the portable screen be relocated within any given milieu, be it the office, home, the car or the bus, but it is even further remote from the background – there is a greater spatio-temporal disconnection. There is a further alienation of the spectator, a further privatization of those techniques, be it the home cinema, portable DVD players, full color display mobile phones. Today vision is fragmented, dislocated, fleeting, flickering, inattentive, diachronic.

Crary's thorough analysis grounds the beginning of today's perceptual world in the nineteenth century, not so much because of the invention of photography and cinema, but rather as the status of the spectator

[1] Ibid., 21–22.

evolved according to "imperatives for consumption, attention, and perceptual competence"[1]

If vision was then relocated from nature into the body, and specifically in the eye, today vision can be pinpointed in the brain. As our knowledge and understanding of the human body is expanded and refined, so too our theories and reflexions must take into account these changes as they open up new areas of relations and possibilities of thought. "Many of the theoretical issues defined in the eighteenth and nineteenth centuries are still not resolved, and they persist despite great advances in the twentieth century in techniques for manipulating visual stimulation.[2]

---

[1] Ibid., 7.

[2] Nicholas J. Wade and Michael T. Swanton, *Visual Perception: an Introduction* (Hove, PA: Psychology Press, 2001), 266.

In Focus

"How everything would be more limpid in our philosophy if we could exorcise those specters, turn them into illusions or objectless perceptions, in the margins of an unequivocal world!"[1]
M. Merleau-Ponty

The state of images

Images surround us to such an extent that it wouldn't be too far fetched to say that we are images and images are us, since our main relation to the world, spiritual and physical, is an iconological one. The constructions we have established in order to manage this relation have evolved through the ages according to our knowledge of the human body and to our technical achievements. Our sense of sight – a most responsible agent but not the only one involved in the formation of representations – is so inborn, our ability to see so taken for granted, it is undisputed that "we see", that we *de facto* consider ourselves image literate when in fact the process of learning "to read" images never occurrs. This is contrary to our faculty of speech. If communicating by sound is also an innate capacity, talking is not an inborn feature; it is a culturally acquired capacity. When we relate words to images we do not stress this difference enough. If seeing is also

[1] Maurice Merleau-Ponty, *L'œil et l'esprit*, Folio essais (Paris: Editions Gallimard, 1964), 36. My translation. « *Comme tout serait plus limpide dans notre philosophie si l'on pouvait exorciser ces spectres, en faire des illusions ou des perceptions sans objet, en marge d'un monde sans équivoque !* »

culturally developed, we have established that we see what we know, we see mainly according to the normative and historical *culture of seeing*, among which the fairly recent Renaissance principle of perspective: through the window pane, we frame our vision, in and out of focus, we see in terms of grounds, fore and back. Then how can we consider ourselves image literate when the learning process never took place? We learn to talk and to read – still unfortunately not a given to all – but we are up to this day not concerned at all by learning how to read images. Why is this the case? Do we really take for granted that the meaning of an image is universal and accessible to all? Or do we pay witness to the biggest swindle of humanity, which continues to allow for free brain washing. Indeed the magical, subversive power of images works, again, on a mass level.

Originally images explained the texts that people couldn't read, these images were understood because stories, orally transmitted, were known. The stories now forgotten, we are left with images that we do not understand but purely and merely consume on an esthetic level. This is the case for most religious statuary and allegorical paintings, for example. Today a small number of people – art historians, archeologists, iconologists – learn to read images in content and structure, and some others – historians and theologists – learn the full stories, fewer still fully apprehend both stories and structures, and they are thus able to decipher images, but what about the rest of us? Could these literacies be intuitive and happen automatically?

Culturally? Today, most daily images do not encode text any longer, they encode realtime events. We think we know them because we recognize their content, are likely to mistake them for "content itself" and forget that images may not selfsame to the events they represent: that they exist on another level of reality, are a construction of meanings and respond to their own rules and to the context of diffusion and reading, which is different for each individual. How is it to be in Tharir Square for days and how is it to see images of this place and these events on Facebook? Two radically different experiences, visually different experiences. If you are in Tharir Square you are unlikely to have a global view (actually such a possibility exists as you could simultaneously be at the event and look at images of the event on Facebook). Surely there is a form of empathy that arises in the viewing of the remote images, a sense of belonging and of communal understanding that perhaps justifies actions. Such a use of images modifies political decision and action. But it is not the same as living through an event, or even to be retold the story from a first hand source, to learn about it by reading from a second hand account or by seeing live footage. The degree of abstraction that sets into action a reflexion and a thinking process to take place is radically different.

How do we read images today? Is there an analytical process voluntarily taking place or does it all happen automatically – heuristically – and to which degree of our consciousness? Is it completely assimilated?

DOUBLE STATUS OF THE IMAGE – RANCIÈRE

For Jacques Rancière the word "image" can designate two different things, a simple relation resembling an original, a placeholder, and a network of operations producing what we call art or an altering of resemblance.[1] There is a third type of images when art finds this original resemblance, what he calls the "archi-ressemblance." He further identifies three main categories of images – naked images (*images nues*), ostensive images (*images ostentatoires*) and metamorphic images (*images métaphoriques*) – all in the domain of art, differentiating these from social images (*images sociales*) and media images (*images médiatiques*). He admits that none of these types of images can function on their own and that each borrows a bit from the others, because of the undetermined character he believes to be essential to images (*indétermination*). It is impossible to isolate art from social and market imagery and their respective interpretation. It is always the context (*dispositif*) that provides the critical discourse, the background to the reading of images. But this *dispositif* is constantly tested against interruptions, derivations and redispositions.[2] Thus Rancière's serious attempt to categorize and rationalize images is challenged and contradicted by what he sees as their very caracteristics.

I think that this point identifies the most acute problem today: not only are images undetermined but images

[1] Jacques Rancière, *Le destin des images* (Paris: La Fabrique, 2003), 14–15.
[2] Ibid., 31–33.

are more and more generic as the crossover of one type into another is more frequent. Besides, they do not have a specific support, context, framework that could identify them clearly as belonging to one type or another. For instance the all important *dispositif*, be it the museum display or the newspaper page that used to clearly identify the level of reading appropriate, is radically questioned. Today each and every image encountered finds itself in the same form – if we are generous – of a 1024x800 pixelated rectangle on an illuminated screen. This leads to something approaching complete indiscrimination, a single monotonous, flat level of reading. So how to make sense of what is seen, how to identify a predominant discourse? There is a confusion, a happy mishmash into which people indifferently step unknowingly, and not particularly caring to know how to read what. If we do not know how to understand images anymore, is this good or bad? Well, of course the answer to this question rests upon intention and involves a different process of thinking banality. Does such a flat reading allow new possibilities for propaganda or no possibility at all, because it just no longer works? Flusser denies the power of propaganda of technical images exactly for this reason.[1]

Rancière shows how images are undecidable and undetermined, whatever their type. Be they art or not, they need a *dispositif* and there are everywhere disturbances

[1] Vilém Flusser, "Television Image and Political Space in the Light of the Romanian Revolution," Kunsthalle, Budapest, 1990, http://www.youtube.com/watch?v=QFTaY2u4NvI.

to the *dispositif*. So what is important is not the image itself but the relation between images. He warns us to look closely to the set of exchanges between all images. What becomes then necessary is what Rancière calls *imagéité*: the relation between elements and functions.

> This presupposes the existence of an infinite Shop/Library/ Museum where all the films, all the texts, photographs and paintings coexist, and where all could be decomposed in elements given each a triple power: the power of singularity (punctum) of the closed image; the educative value (studium) of the document bearing the traces of a story and the combinatory capacity of the sign, susceptible to associate with any element from another series to compose to infinity new image-sentences.[1]

This utopia that Rancière described a few years ago exists nowadays. But it is not clear to what extent we are aware of it, and whether we are making the right connections; if we have the necessary distance to see it, recognize it and make use of it properly; but the potential is surely there.

About photography, Rancière says that it "became art because it plays on a double poetic of the image: it is

---

[1] Rancière, *Le destin des images*, 39. My translation. « Cela suppose l'existence d'un Magasin/Bibliothèque/Musée infini où tous les films, tous les textes, les photographies et les tableaux coexistent, et où tous soient décomposables en éléments dotés chacun d'une triple puissance: la puissance de singularité (le punctum) de l'image obtuse; la valeur d'enseignement (le studium) du document portant la trace d'une histoire et la capacité combinatoire du signe, susceptible de s'associer avec n'importe quel élément d'une autre série pour composer à l'infini de nouvelles phrases-images. »

both the code of a history written in visible forms and a mute reality (obtuse), the document of a history written on faces and a pure bloc of visibility."[1]
The "pensive image" (*image pensive*) is the image that would carry in itself the potentiality of thinking. It is by definition the indeterminate characteristic of the photographic image, which is "full of thoughts unthought." "The pensive character of photography could thus be defined as a knot between several indeterminations. [...] The pensive character of the image, it is the latent presence of one level of expression in another."[2]
Here again we can draw the parallel with Flusser's quantum characteristics of the image, which is in two states at once.
This permeability and malleability of images in their electronic form provides a platform of anticipation and creation. To paraphrase Rancière, the new relations thus established can only be defined by the spectator; it is his gaze that gives reality to the equilibrium between the metamorphosis of electronic matter and the staging of a century's history.[3]

Rancière refers to Godard's *Histoires du cinéma* in order to demonstrate the power of "this surface on which all the images can slide one on top of the other" thanks to the "fraternity of metaphors which is based on this

[1] Ibid., 20. My translation.

[2] Jacques Rancière, *Le spectateur émancipé* (Paris: La Fabrique, 2008), 132. My translation.

[3] Ibid., 137. My translation. « C'est le spectateur seul qui peut fixer la mesure du rapport, c'est son seul regard qui donne réalité à l'équilibre entre les métamorphoses de la 'matière' informatique et la mise en scène de l'histoire d'un siècle. »

double power of each image: to condensate a multiplicity of gesture significant of a time and to associate itself with all the images doted of the same power."[1]

> This rapport of an art to itself by the mediation of an other [...] this notion of "pensiveness" that designates in the image something that resist to thoughts, to the thought of the one who made it and the one who tries to identify it. [...] This resistance is not a constitutive property of the nature of some images, but a play of gaps between several function-images present on the same surface.[2]

And this will be increasingly so, as he further points out that new technologies will only offer new possibilities for metamorphoses and juxtapositions, so that the image is increasingly "pensive."

Rancière's analyses of the status of images, even though he focuses mainly on the register of art, can be applied to all images – especially as the borders between art and non-art, as he himself stresses, are increasingly thin and permeable. The image is primarily undetermined, it needs a context or what is refered to as a *dispositif* to be interpreted, it is double always, both a historic document and a bloc of visibility. By nature it can be thought, it is pensive; it has an

---

[1] Ibid., 138. My translation.

[2] Ibid., 139. My translation. « Ce rapport d'un art à lui-même par la médiation d'un autre [...] cette notion de pensivité qui désigne dans l'image quelque chose qui résiste à la pensée, à la pensée de celui qui l'a produite et de celui qui cherche à l'idenifier. [...] cette résistance [...] n'est pas une propriété constitutive de la nature de certaines images, mais un jeu d'écarts entre plusieurs fonctions-images présentes sur la même surface. »

extraordinary power to encompass other levels of understanding, of resistance.

IMAGE AS A SITE OF RESISTANCE – DIDI-HUBERMAN

In a precious little book entitled *La survivance des Lucioles*, Didi-Huberman contributes to understanding the relation between Walter Benjamin's conception of the image as a gesture of remembrance and his own conception of images as the ultimate site of resistance.

Writing about the intermittent character of photography, which is fundamental according to Denis Roche, he makes clear links to Walter Benjamin: "How, here not to think about the spasmodic character of the dialectical image according to Walter Benjamin, this notion precisely destined to understand in which way *the times become visible*, how history appears to us in a passing lightening that must be named image?"[1] It is this flickering capacity that allows the image to last, to disappear where challenged and reappear again somewhere else but not to go away. Digital images have this characteristic inscribed in them: they can be turned on and off. Like fireflies (*lucioles*), images can resist the artificial omnipresent surveillance and control of the spotlights, but unlike Pasolini who lost hope, Didi-Huberman

[1] Georges Didi-Huberman, *Survivance des lucioles* (Paris: Editions de Minuit, 2009), 38. My translation. « Comment, ici ne pas penser au caractère 'saccadé' de l'image dialectique selon Walter Benjamin, cette notion précisement destinée à comprendre de quelle façon *les temps se font visibles*, comment l'histoire même nous apparaît en un éclair passager qu'il faut nommer 'image'? »

believes in the survival of the fireflies and therefore calls to "[...] rethink our own 'principle of hope' through the way in which the Once encounters the Now to form a glow, a sparkle, a constellation where some form is liberated for our own Future."[1]

Philosophical extrapolations

PHENOMENOLOGY – MERLEAU-PONTY

It is through vision that we primarily relate to the world-out-there, and it is vision that has enabled the development of a phenomenological method of philosophy from Plato to Kant to Husserl and Heidegger. But if what we see has been the determinative factor in understanding how we think, how we see what we see has been our preoccupation. The question has now shifted to what it is exactly that we see and how it is changing what we think of it. Joohan Kim, of the Yonsei University of Seoul, starts to ask pertinent questions in the *Phenomenology of Digital-Being*. Here I would like to apply one of his considerations to photography and the technical image, in light of a few of Merleau-Ponty's remarks on the relation between vision and the body of the seer.

---

[1] Ibid., 51. My translation. « [...] repenser notre prope 'principe d'espérance' à travers la façon dont l'Autrefois rencontre le Maintenant pour former une lueur, un éclat, une constellation où se libère quelque forme pour notre Avenir lui-même. »

In *L'œil et l'esprit*, Merleau-Ponty brings back the body in the mind:

> It is by lending his body to the world that the painter changes the world in painting. To understand these transubstantiations, it is necessary to find again the operating and actual body that is not a piece of space, a beam of functions that is a weaving of vision and movement. [...] My mobile body accounts to the visible world, is part of it, and that is why I can direct it in the visible. Furthermore it is true too that vision is suspended to movement. One sees only what one looks at. [...] The visible world and the world of my motorized projects are total parts of the same Being.[1]

Vision, body and movement are conditionally linked in the grasping of the world out there. So how does the habitus or lifeworld that is induced here by Merleau-Ponty comprehend images of it that are unbound by spacio-temporal coordinates? Indeed, as Kim points out, if Heidegger tells us "in perception, the perceived entity is bodily there", then what do we perceive when looking at an image on a screen which has a certain 'bodily presence' without 'being bodily-there' at all?[2]

---

[1] Merleau-Ponty, *L'œil et l'esprit*, 16. My translation. « C'est en prêtant son corps au monde que le peintre change le monde en peinture. Pour comprendre ces transsubstanciations, il faut retrouver le corps opérant et actuel, celui qui n'est pas un morceau d'espace, un faisceau de fonctions, qui est un entrelacs de vision et de mouvement. [...] Mon corps mobile compte au monde visible, en fait partie, et c'est pourquoi je peux le diriger dans le visible. Par ailleurs il est vrai aussi que la vision est suspendue au mouvement. On ne voit que ce qu'on regarde. [...] Le monde visible et celui de mes projets moteurs sont des parties totales du meme Être. »

[2] Joohan Kim, "Phenomenology of Digital-Being," *Human Studies* no. 24 (2001): 94.

Today the visible world greatly exceeds the potentialities of a bodily being but continues to give her the illusion of presence. It is this gap that enters into play when one is looking at cell phone images of the Arab Spring in Tharir Square. Flusser had grasped this transition from one level of reality to the next when he wrote in a text on politics and the technical image in 1990 that there is no longer an ontological problem when images are in power, because what is concrete is in the image, and all the rest is metaphysical.[1]

THE MONAD'S EYE – DELEUZE/LEIBNIZ/BENJAMIN

The monad is a simple substance without parts, a perpetual living mirror of the universe, responding to appetition and perception principles. According to Leibniz and as famously reported by Deleuze, the monad also has no window and no door; it is a completely self-contained entity that contains all. But the monad has a "clear zone" (*la zone claire*), and this zone is linked to the body. This zone is a mirror-like surface that reflects the world; it is the site where understanding happens. It is the eye. The image also has no opening and it contains the world.

> Once more, since the world does not exist outside of the monads, these are small objectless perceptions, hallucinatory microperceptions. The world exists only in its representatives as they are included in each monad. [...] It is as

[1] Vilém Flusser, "Le politique à l'age des images techniques (1990)," in *La civilisation des médias* (Belval, France: Circé, 2006), 125.

> if the bottom of each monad was constituted of an infinity of small folds (inflexions) that don't stop folding and unfolding in all directions, [...] And it is those small, obscure, confused perceptions that compose our macroperceptions, our conscious, clear and distinct apperceptions [...][1]

In a theory of the monad, there is no longer a need to distinguish between the mind and the body. The monad perceives through its body, and the body has monads that in turn have their own body. These second monads have bodies filled with monads that have bodies: mind and body are distinct but inseparable.[2] There is underlying here a quantum aspect of the structure of the monad. Besides monads are always actual and they refer to virtualities that they actualize in a perpetual stream.[3] Finally, there is only perception inside the monad and the phenomenon is the perceived, which has a double structure and is the result of an unconscious psychical mechanism.[4]

"Thinking involves not only the movement of thoughts, but their arrest as well. Where thinking suddenly comes

---

[1] Gilles Deleuze, *Le pli: Leibniz et le Baroque* (Paris: Éditions de Minuit, 1988), 114–115. My translation. « Encore une fois, le monde n'existant pas hors des monads, ce sont de petites perceptions sans objet, des microperceptions hallucinatoires. Le monde n'existe que dans ses représentants tels qu'ils sont inclus dans chaque monade. [...] C'est comme si le fond de chaque monade était constitué d'une infinité de petits plis (inflexions) qui ne cessent de se faire et de se défaire en toutes directions, [...] Et ce sont ces petites perceptions obscures, confuses, qui composent nos macroperceptions, nos aperceptions conscientes, claires et distinctes [...] »

[2] Ibid., 144–145.

[3] Ibid., 109.

[4] Ibid., 126.

to a stop in a constellation saturated with tensions, it gives that constellation a shock, by which thinking is crystallized as a monad. The historical materialist approaches a historical object only where it confronts him as a monad."[1] Benjamin's idea of the monad is a dialectical image that requires a visual logic in order to imagine and construct the objects of history.

L'image-trou as I would like to call it – the 'peeping' image or image-hole – sees inside itself beyond appearances. It is the supra-technical image; an image on steroids so to speak, as it combines simultaneously several sources of information or informations, which are recombined according to metacodes. The most vivid example is the 4D medical image, whose powers are fully exposed with tools such as the open-source Osyrix software.[2] It enjoys looking at its own world as it has its own capacity to see. It is not simulation but something of the order of the supra-real, a pure visual construction. It is the monad of the homogenerator.

Incorporeality

The corporeal character of images have defined their status for the longest part of history from cave paintings to funerary masks, from frescos on church walls to court portraiture, from drip paintings to newsreels.

---

[1] Walter Benjamin, *Selected Writings Volume 4 1938-1940*, trans. Edmund Jephcott (Cambridge, MA: The Belknapp Press, 2006), 396 (Thesis XVII) .

[2] http://www.osirix-viewer.com/

If photography could have been the medium to liberate images from the fixity of a support by enhancing their reproducibility and multiplying their ubiquity, photography is in fact the process that materializes light, gives it body. So the incorporeality of images only appears with their translation into the binary abstraction of the digital code, when light is reduced to a sequence of 0-1 that is fully transportable, ubiquitous, multiple to the infinite. An image is now simultaneously an electric medium and pure energy (perhaps as far as energy is matter, we could debate about a physical presence of some sorts).

THE SYNTHETIC IMAGE – FLUSSER

According to Flusser, words and images at some point were no longer sufficient to conceptualize the world. There was a need for new codes to calculate the world, as "numbers are the images of thoughts." Synthetic images, being the numbers transcoded into digital code, in turn transcoded into images by the computer, thus came to provide a much needed and clearer understanding of concepts. But these technical images require a new kind of thinking, "systemic or structural," that must start by taking into account "images as articulation of thoughts."[1]

[1] Flusser, "Television Image and Political Space in the Light of the Romanian Revolution."

The invention of photography reintroduces images within texts out from which Guttenberg's press had expelled them. Technical images were supposed to reintroduce magic into the texts and make them comprehensible anew but rather than reintroducing images into daily life, they displace them, rather than explaining texts they translate scientific statements.

Technical images are metacodes that have turned culture into mass-culture. As long as the mode of transmission of these images was unilateral, they could only fulfill their "function of programming behavior" and transform those who receive them into objects. But as soon as the possibility of a network and the multilateral exchanges of images appear, they become a new immaterial surface onto which new significations can be projected by many participants at once. Images become vectors of signification.[1] They take on their full potential of an immaterial and pure surface onto which all preceding images can be transported, transcoded.[2]

Unlike the precedent technical revolution, which transformed the body, these new techniques stimulate the nervous system; they are virtual. There is no reality behind the image. All reality is in the image.

[1] Vilém Flusser, *La civilisation des médias* (Belval, France: Circé, 2006), 73–74.
[2] Ibid., 69.

The vision machine – a completely autonomous sightless vision apparatus as described by Virilio in his eponymous book – points ironically to the "factual nature of our own mental images." The relevant question is thus no longer about their objectivity, since it is established, but about their reality and in turn the "paradoxical facticity of the instrumental virtual images." There is confusion, Virilio claims, between the factual – images that operate – and the virtual as the 'reality effect' is taking over the reality principle. The moment the retinal image is memorized the "paradoxically real nature of 'virtual imagery' was in fact posed." The objectification of the image is thus independent from any kind of *support-surface,* that is of a material present in space. It is now linked to time: the time of exposure.[1]

Additionally, if every image is the manifestation of energy, then retinal retention is more than the lasting imprint of the retina but "the intensive time of human perceptiveness."[2] The entire question of vision is shifted from a relation to space to a relation in time. In this perspective, we must keep the following lines in mind in trying to understand the effects (and affects) of our contemporary visual environment:

---

[1] Paul Virilio, *The Vision Machine* (Bloomington, IN: Indiana University Press, 1994), 60–61.

[2] Ibid., 75.

All that is still *fixed* is in fact threatened by this 'panoptical inertia' of the speed of light in the void; of these electromagnetic waves that derealize the work of the optical radiation of the day, to the profit of the sole electro-optical radiation of the false day of the screens. [...] How to resist effectively to the sudden derealization of a world where all is sight – already seen and instantaneously forgotten? [1]

1 Paul Virilio, *L'art à perte de vue* (Paris: Galilée, 2005), 108. My translation. « Tout ce qui est encore *fixe* est de fait menacé par cette «inertie panoptique» de la vitesse de la lumière dans le vide; de ces ondes électromagnétiques qui déréalisent l'œuvre du rayonnement optique du jour, au profit du seul rayonnement électro-optique du faux jour des écrans. [...] Comment résister efficacement à la soudaine déréalisation d'un monde où tout est vue - deja vu et instantanément oublié? »

Pix, Bits and Qbits

Flusser's quantum analogies

> The act of photography is that of 'phenomenological doubt', to the extent that it attempts to approach phenomena from any number of viewpoints. [...] Ultimately, there is a final decision taken in the act of photography: pressing the shutter release [...]. In reality, however, these final decisions are only the last of a series of part-decisions resembling grains of sand [...]. As consequently, no decision is really 'decisive', but part of a series of clear and distinct quantum-decisions, likewise only a series of photographs can testify to the photographer's intention. [...] The structure of the act of photography is a quantum one: a doubt made up of points of hesitation and points of decision-making.[1]

The entire photographic universe is deeply rooted in a quantum-like structure, not only the act of taking a photograph per se. Photographs are grainy, they are made of little pieces of information which can be independently modified to alter the whole picture; they are made in series. And additionally the entire process of photography from capturing to rendering is entirely calculable, since it is the product of the camera, itself a Flusserian program. The following work of selecting images is again one of choices among series of images. And the results of this act of photography is that images,

[1] Flusser, *Towards a Philosophy of Photography*, 38–39.

technical images are surrounding us from all sides, their "presence is ubiquitous."[1]

Photographs encode concepts, become models and transmit information. It is thus crucial to be able to decode photographs in order to read and understand the photographic message, if not "they remain undecoded" and can "accomplish their task perfectly: programming society to act as though under a magic spell."[2]

Flusser's description of photography as a quantum system applies to everything that is linked to an apparatus, a calculating machine as he defines it, and all that is characteristic of the post-industrial age. He extends this conception to the individuals themselves, stating that there can no longer be an individual, since all divisible: "The human being can no longer be seen as an individual but rather as the opposite, as a dense scattering of parts; he is calculable."[3]

Thus we can no longer describe the world in written and spoken words as they are no longer appropriate to describe the bits that form it, but as they are calculable the world can be represented in images again. "To imagine it, we must mobilize a power of imagination that rests upon calculation. [...] Contemporary

[1] Ibid., 40.

[2] Ibid., 48.

[3] Vilém Flusser, "The City as Wave-Trough in the Image-Flood," trans. Phil Gochenour, *Critical Inquiry* 31, no. 2 (2005): 320–328. The text is dated 1988, it was given as a conference in 1989 and first published in German in 1990.

relations among human beings will increasingly encode themselves into images of this type. Our perspectives, imaginings, emotions, intentions, knowledge, and decisions must increasingly assume the form of such images."

Martin's objective model for thoughts

In the fields of physics and psychiatry, researchers are also looking to find ways of explaining and describing the world we know in different terms. To this end François Martin, physicist at the University of Paris 6, Federico Carminati, physicist at CERN and Giuliana Galli Carminati, chief doctor at the Mental Development Psychiatry Unit at the Geneva University Hospital, propose a quantum theory of consciousness; using a quantum model, they explain theories such as synchronicity. If the claims they make are perfectly calculable and already verified at the level of the infinitely small, they remain speculative on a larger scale, even if experience abounds. The parallels between hypotheses proposed in science, psychology and philosophy are too close not to follow them.

Almost a century ago, Carl Jung justified the events of synchronicity with his theory of the *unus mundus*, a One World from where everything originates and returns, and which can be related to Plato's concept of the World of Ideas. Martin draws parallels from these theories to quantum physics as "the unus mundus underlies both mind and matter."[1] What is crucial to understand is that "there is no causal link between correlated events localized in space and time" in a synchronic effect. In consequence synchronicity cannot be explained by classical physics, whereas psychic coincidences can be explained via analogy with quantum entanglement and it is possible to see "synchronistic events between the mental and the material domains as a consequence of a quantum entanglement between mind and matter." In plainer language, this refers to the notion that something like chance is not the effect of hazard. What can appear as pure luck, a coincidence, is in fact the result of a calculable encounter, in a world where "mind and matter are unseparated", and the mental and the material are "manifestations of one underlying reality."[2]

If synchronicity phenomena exist and if we accept the possibility of "the projection of our subjectivity in the environment"[3], then mental states cannot be reduced to physical states of the brain; they are only correlated. The individual is not bound by space-time and the reality of the object lies in the observation of the subject.

These considerations contribute to Flusser's call to build new systems of thinking about the nature of the technical image and its situation (role) within these

---

[1] François Martin, Federico Carminati, and Giuliana Galli Carminati, "Synchronicity, Quantum Information and the Psyche," *Journal of Cosmology* 3 (2009): 580–589.
[2] Ibid.
[3] Ibid.

very propositions. For example, let us take into account and keep in mind that the Bose-Einstein condensation is a phenomenon "in which each particle loses its individuality in favour of a collective, global behaviour."[1]

Jung's collective unconscious

There is an enduring misconception of archetypes as having a specific content, as if they were unconscious representations. In order to clarify his conception, Jung insisted that an "archetype in itself is empty, it is a pure formal element, nothing more than a *facultas praeformandi* (a possibility of pre-formation), a form of representation given *a priori*."[2]

As a primary image, the archetype acquires a specified content when it becomes conscious and is filled with the material of conscious experience. Basically an archetype is purely formal, nothing else but a pre-shaping possibility or an innate tendency of shaping things. Thus it is impossible to explain or to "solve" an archetype. Martin compares a quantum field to an archetype, as both do not have a material existence, "they only exist as Potentia."[3]

---

[1] Ibid.

[2] Carl Gustav Jung, *Les racines de la conscience* (Paris: Buchet-Chastel, 1971), 167; François Martin, "Mécanique Quantique et Psychisme," Conférence au Département de psychiatrie des Hôpitaux universitaires de Genève 12 Février 2009.

[3] Martin, "Mécanique quantique et psychisme."

The same could be said about the digital image. Even though it always has content, the code this content resides in remains hidden until its form appears when it is decoded onto the screen. The rest of the time, when it is stored, rendered, processed or travelling on the network, it is also in potentiality.

Jung's idea of the collective unconscious is a vacuum that contains archetypes: "It is the state of possibility of all the psychic qualities and attributes of the Universe, all the laws and structure of the physical Universe."[1] And it is available directly to an individual unconscious: "We can assert that an individual unconscious 'knows everything', in the sense that any individual unconscious has access to any information in the Universe."[2]
This Jungian model "could be similar to what happens in quantum field theory of matter in which vacuum permeates all space-time and all matter"[3]. Martin et al. have thus "postulated the existence of an underlying universal mental (unconscious and consciousness) quantum field. It appears that it is a quantum interpretation, in terms of quantum fields, of the layered model of the Collective Unconscious that Jung gave in 1925."[4]

---

[1] Belal E. Baaquie and François Martin, "Quantum Psyche. Quantum Field Theory of the Human Psyche," *NeuroQuantology* 3, no. 1 (2005): 7–42.

[2] François Martin, Federico Carminati, and Giuliana Galli Carminati, "Comments on a Quantum Model of the Psyche," April 2011, 5–6.

[3] Ibid., 6.

[4] Ibid., 27.

Jung has described the inner images from the unconscious as a stream. If we draw parallels between the pool or stream of images described by Jung that reside in our unconscious, the model proposed by Martin of an underlying mental quantum field and the cloud of more or less dense bits that constitute the alternative worlds of Flusser, we can begin to make fruitful connections between these complementary systems of thinking.

The Darkroom

The darkroom is a magical, somber place of solitude, where the photographer, in the intimacy of her own presence, manufactures images one by one, where the captured luminous essence of an image comes into existence as a physical printed image. It is a place that has vanished. The ones that remain, untouched, abandoned, left behind with the keen hope of being used some time again, keep the acrid smell of the chemicals turned sour in the bottom of plastic gallon jars. Old darkrooms look like an ancient site of almost forgotten pagan rituals... places of transformations, the place of the alchemist. What survives today is the black box of the camera, still mysterious (perhaps even more so) as it excludes the possibility of being inside. Inside the camera, it is now the place where it all happens at once, the capture and its simultaneous translation into something else that is revealed instantaneously in broad daylight in the illuminations of its screen.

The darkroom was a place of active creation, of transmutation, of experimentations that were governed by thinking processes, volition, purpose, intentions; with its disappearance the transformation is left to the machine; it is automated. The thinking process is gone and the responsibility of creation gone with it. Symbolically, this reflection has to happen somewhere else, and for lack of a better place, the following pages provides us with a makeshift darkroom.

In the flux of images and the choice of sources on output, the moments spent at the museum or with an illustrated monthly in hand are becoming rare as they require not only taking the time involved in solely indulging such activities but additionally the time requested by the emotional thinking process stimulated by said activities. Thus the primary source of cultural and informational input is delivered directly by the stream. Indeed who is interested in reading a story when there is a thousand interconnecting stories being told at once, and all of these available simultaneously. Following the advice of my teacher Wolfgang Schirmacher and his invitation to "be courageous enough to use your own voice", the following chapter lays out intuitions that are at the beginning of their development.

Theory of fasciae[1]

Fasciae are found everywhere in the human body, at every level, just beneath the surface and at its deepest core, enabling rapid survival responses, protecting and permitting most vital functions to happen. An uninterrupted three-dimensiomal web of tissue, they are responsible to make the body work as a whole and not

[1] In order to cut short any misinterpretations, let me stress that the word fascia directly originates ethymologically from the latin *fascia, ae* meaning a band, bandage, ribbon, such as the long narrow fabric that was used to envelop newborns, and must not be linked, despite its apparent close homonymie, to *fascis, es* meaning bundle, describing the Roman instrument of power and its symbol and which gave the italian word *fascio, sci* the league that refers to political groups, a number of which evolved in to fascism.

just as an assembly of parts. They fill unoccupied space and as a kind of binding agent, they transport the information that assures intercellular communication. In medicine they are credited most often for their malfunctions, when the visceral fasciae get inflammed – peritonitis, meningitis, pleurisy – or when deep fasciae break – torn ligaments – but are rarely acknowledged for their fundamental and generally ceaseless accomplishments.

One image holds all possible images. The sheer combination of the digital information contained in a file is virtually infinite, although according to Flusser, the number of the possibilities of the program "is large but nevertheless finite".[1] It is the composition of the image that is one and all; it is a perpetual arrangement.

Photography today is fluid. It is transient, modular and ubiquitous. It stands with certainty at the opposite of any idea of fixation. Hence, the by now old Barthian notion of a "ça a été" must irreversibly be replaced in our understanding and reading of photography by a "c'est", an "it has been" versus an "it is", the past tense traded for a simple present. Thus a photograph is always now, in becoming never a witness of the past but only one construction of many other possible constructions.

This is permitted by the disappearance of its longtime *support*, paper, which has been replaced by electricity.

[1] Flusser, *Towards a Philosophy of Photography*, 26.

I use here the French word which indicates more precisely the role that the paper format had in carrying images, whereas the correct English word *medium* is more appropriate to describe the current role of the screen, which does not "support" anything but merely transmits. The screen is a mediator, a transmitter of information not a carrier of information. In fact, the image doesn't sit on the screen; it resides either in the light diodes, the liquid crystals or in the ionised gas cells of the screen, and is in no way fixed on it. The screen remains an interface to view the image but in no way its permanent *support*. The dematerialization of the image is thus complete. This is, in turn, what allows the image to "float" as so many particles in thin air, in a flux that is totally still while constantly streaming; it can be here, there, nowhere and everywhere at once. And it is. And exactly so too, it is in our mind.

It is this immobile seamless stream that I propose to compare by analogy to physical fasciae. The fasciae are a continuous connective tissue allowing movement but not in movement themselves. It is a network for the passage of information, an extended idea of the fabric present outside the human body, everywhere in the outer physical world. This is how the world is interconnected, through a thin veil of energy, forming a tissue of information around all beings and things, from and to beings and things, like a dense network of communication fibers. There is no unoccupied space, fasciae fill the void. There are the channels of interactions and what allows ideas to flow freely, and with causality, around and pass from matter to matter, from one side of the globe to the other. These fasciae comply with the law of energy conservation. I would venture to say that this place, momentarily called the fasciae, is where this visual energy (the image) is ultimately stored.

Digital images are suspended images, on the surface of our desktop they scroll and roll and paradoxically, in a Godardian way, follow one another, not replacing but adding to each other, to fabricate a boundless single image extending beyond our potential field of vision into the atmosphere.

Cartography 1:1

The infinite series of curvatures or inflexions, it is the world, and the entire world is included in the soul under one point of view.[1]
G. Deleuze

Images now function on one single level: the televisual level of the screen. There is no sense of scale that is possible any longer since all images take the standard format of the computer screen. Paradoxically though, the sheer abundance of these small rectangles overlapping each other is turning Borges' allegorical story about the uselessness of an exact science into a reality. "In time, those Unconscionable Maps no longer satisfied, and the Cartographers Guilds struck a Map of the

[1] Deleuze, *Le pli: Leibniz et le Baroque*, 34. My translation. « La série infinie des courbures ou inflexions, c'est le monde, et le monde entier est inclus dans l'âme sous un point de vue. »

Empire whose size was that of the Empire, and which coincided point for point with it."[1]

Blaise Aguera y Arcas, founder of Seadragon, "a web optimized visualization technology that allows graphics and photos to be smoothly browsed, regardless of their size,"[2] acquired by Microsoft and used for its Bing mapping service, developed a software called Photosynth. It is "a powerful set of tools for capturing and viewing the world in 3D"[3] "that analyzes digital photographs and generates a three-dimensional model of the photos and a point cloud of a photographed object. Pattern recognition components compare portions of images to create points, which are then compared to convert the image into a model. Users are able to view and generate their own models using a software tool available for download at the Photosynth website."[4] In fewer words, these elaborate algorithms create a seamless mapping of the world the size of the world, albeit one that fits into a pocket. It is a complete social interactive environment, a duplication – or is it a fold? – built on shared collective memories. Our memories today are no longer solely indexed by our hippocampus, but most often are retrievable through

---

[1] Jorge Borges, *Collected Stories* (London: Allenlanethe Penguin Press, 2004), 159.

[2] Wikipedia contributors, "Seadragon Software," *Wikipedia, the Free Encyclopedia* (Wikimedia Foundation, Inc., July 26, 2012), http://en.wikipedia.org/w/index.php?title=Seadragon_Software&oldid=504212999.

[3] http://photosynth.net/about.aspx/.

[4] Wikipedia contributors, "Photosynth," *Wikipedia, the Free Encyclopedia* (Wikimedia Foundation, Inc., August 15, 2012), http://en.wikipedia.org/w/index.php?title=Photosynth&oldid=504647379.

the Finder of our computers amongst the thousands of digital snapshots that vouch for our existence and compensate for what seems to be an increasing deficiency in remembrance. In this vast landscape, another big large telecoms company, Cisco, is ensuring that humans have a TelePresence of their own and fit exactly in the place they are supposed to inhabit. What exactly are the semantic links in these global interconnections?

I am grateful to William J. Mitchell for bringing back to my attention an incredibly foresighted text by Oliver Wendell Holmes written as early as 1859 for the journal *The Atlantic*. Unfortunately, Mitchell quoted Holmes along with Sontag to make a point against the proliferation of photographic images as "a sinister ally of the late-capitalist state"[1] that has presumably accelerated with digital imaging. If a study of the relation of capitalism to the evolution of the technical image is of interest, the quote misrendered Holmes enthusiastic disposition toward photography and his fascinating prescience. We will quote him at length here to let him speak for himself:

> Form is henceforth divorced from matter. In fact, matter as a visible object is of no great use any longer, except as the mould on which form is shaped. Give us a few negatives of a thing worth seeing, taken from different points of view, and that is all we want of it. Pull it down or burn it up, if you please. We must, perhaps, sacrifice some luxury in the

[1] Mitchell, *The Reconfigured Eye. Visual Truth in the Post-photographic Era*, 56.

loss of color; but form and light and shade are the great things, and even color can be added, and perhaps by and by may be got direct from Nature.
There is only one Coliseum or Pantheon; but how many millions of potential negatives have they shed, —representatives of billions of pictures, —since they were erected! Matter in large masses must always be fixed and dear; form is cheap and transportable. We have got the fruit of creation now, and need not trouble ourselves with the core. Every conceivable object of Nature and Art will soon scale its surface for us. Men will hunt all curious, beautiful, grand objects, as they hunt the cattle in South America, for their skins, and leave the carcasses as of little worth.

The consequence of this will soon be such an enormous collection of forms that they will have to be classified and arranged in vast libraries, as books are now. The time will come when a man who wishes to see any object, natural or artificial, will go to the Imperial, National, or City Stereographic Library and call for its skin or form, as he would for a book at any common library. We do now distinctly propose the creation of a comprehensive and systematic stereographic library, where all men can find the special forms they particularly desire to see as artists, or as scholars, or as mechanics, or in any other capacity. Already a workman has been travelling about the country with stereographic views of furniture, showing his employer's patterns in this way, and taking orders for them. This is a mere hint of what is coming before long.[1]

---

[1] Oliver Wendell Holmes, "The Stereoscope and the Stereograph," *The Atlantic*, June 1859, http://www.theatlantic.com/magazine/archive/1859/06/the-stereoscope-and-the-stereograph/3361/.

Social implications

In 1888 when Eastman Kodak claimed "You press the button we do the rest", it was the first mass diffusion of the practice of photography that would revolutionize the way we remember and live and see. Today's paradigmatic shift to the digital is harder to pinpoint to a specific date. The advent of the cheap digital camera together with the proliferation of online social networks might have a slogan like "You do it all", since the entire chain of image production and diffusion is in the hands of the image capturer. Or alternatively, "You do nothing at all", because where is the personnal or individual authorship in picture making today: isn't the machine doing it all anyway?

Images have indeed surpassed the biological body of the nineteenth century for they exist and are consumed solely or conditionally within an environmental context. There is no end of history and no justification for an additional classification of photography into a post-practice as Tomas suggests. On the contrary, our historical referential system is shifting from a linear to a circular or rhizomatic or perhaps a folding kind of system, with the multiplication of focus zones as different states of consciousness. There is no longer a *moi-sujet* versus a *world-objet* but a dissolution of the I into the world.

Getty Images owns 70 millions images and amongst them are the most famous and historically important that exist. Getty's CEO, Jonathan Klein, believes that images have the power to question our core beliefs, that they have a power to change the world, to make government act in case of disasters, for example, or in case of wars.[1] Facebook reports to store over 90 billions of images on its servers with an additional upload rate of 250 million images per day, a high proportion of which constitute the most mundane and redundant image set ever produced.[2]
What power do these images have? Who do they serve? Who manipulates them, produces them, provides access to them? The answer used to be unequivocal: mass media. But it is no longer so black and white as the general public has never before been both the producer and consumer of images often under Free Documentation or Creative Commons licenses or those directly in the public domain. Nevertheless, since the channels of diffusion are proprietary, the network itself is a total control mechanism for the storage and the access of whatever powers these images yield. It is not clear who owns what in the very end.

In the analogue era, access points were limited, and controlled geographically and linguistically, through books, newspapers, magazines, television and cinema,

---

[1] http://www.ted.com/talks/jonathan_klein_photos_that_changed_the_world.html

[2] http://www.quora.com/How-many-photos-are-uploaded-to-Facebook-each-day and http://mashable.com/2011/10/21/facebook-infographic/

which diffused carefully selected images made by a professional class for their targeted audience. In the digital world, the access points are multiple and unlimited, the diversity of materials and the quality thereof is incommensurable: all merge into an indistinguishable mass readily at hand, with the advantage of being available but with the greater challenge of having to sort the good from the bad. Does this inform people in developing their greater sense of diversity and in sharpening their own selective taste towards a finer appreciation? Or does the situation as described average the standard toward the lower end of the scale of what is available?

The speed at which an image is replaced by another one also challenges our faculties of remembrance, which have already been put to test by the sheer facility with which the apparatuses surrounding us remember *for us*. The camera records and stores our most privileged moments for eternity – so that we can forget. In terms of brain plasticity it would be interesting to find out if our ability to remember just diminishes as it is less tested, or whether brain space/power is allocated to processing this increasing amount of information. Are we are becoming creatures who remember less but think more?

Conclusion

Ever since Plato's cave story, mankind has imprisoned herself in the problematics of the images. The invention of photography has made matter more complex by trapping it in another set of ideas about representation, no longer of the order of the imaginary but of the indexical. The shift from analogue to digital imaging and the vast possibilities of discoveries and transmissions that have emerged with these new technologies and networks have exposed us to a complete new set of images to look at, and thus demand of us a complete rethinking of the way we see. The liberation from past conceptions must be total in order to comprehend images' new symbolic and face values.

In this brief presentation, our field of study has broadened to encompass historical as well as scientific concerns. These concerns have to be taken into consideration when addressing the immense question of sight. And hence thought. This essay raises many questions yet to be further developped. In this, our darkroom of ideas on the printed page, we have attempted to pursue new thoughts and indentified pathways, areas worthy of pinning up for further research and those that serve as background to all that will come.

Our flow of consciousness is matched by an equivalent flow of images that we can tap into, uninterrupted.

It is our contemporary condition that it is becoming increasingly difficult to differentiate between image and consciousness at all.

To conclude in Flusser's words:

"The image is the event."[1]

December 2011

[1] Flusser, "Television Image and Political Space in the Light of the Romanian Revolution."

Annex

Therefore, media aesthetics relies on examples from films, video, photography, sound environments and cannot be presented properly without such evidence on display. You have to see, to feel, to appreciate yourself, get hooked und involved - and no philosophical description can replace this personal participation.[1]
Wolfgang Schirmacher

Rather than presenting these images directly as illustrations of the specific arguments discussed in the preceding thesis, I prefer to propose them separately from the text, even though some references are quite straightforward and obvious. The sequence in which they are presenteed is following free associations and thus the reader is invited to form her own associations. The captions are also separated from the images and listed at the end, so that the images can first be fully captured in their pensive character without any textual determination.

---

1 Schirmacher, "Media aesthetics in Europe."

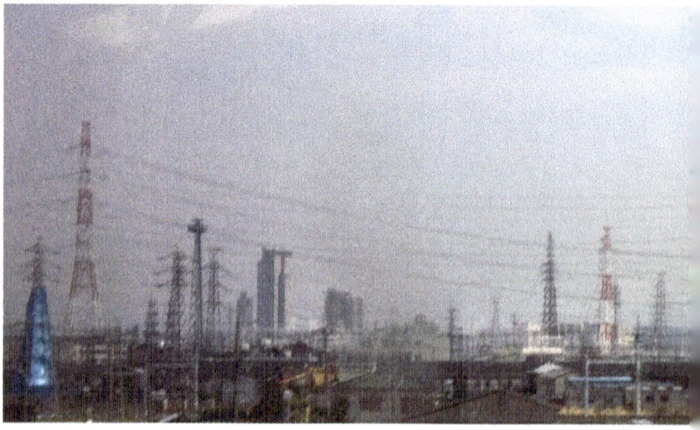

SUN

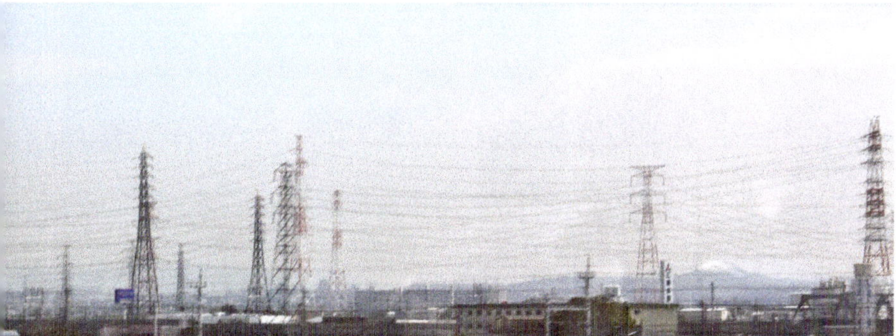

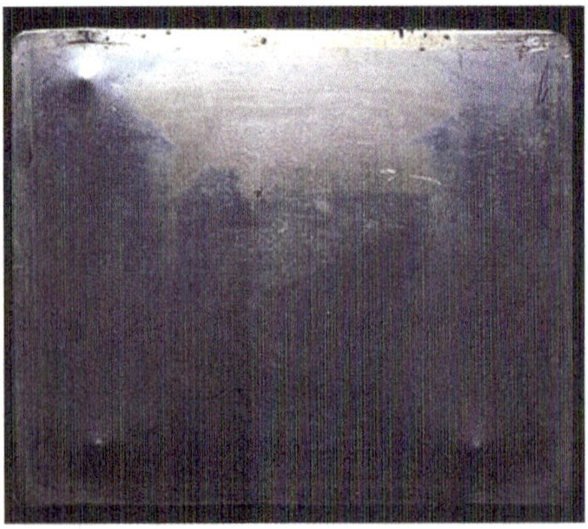

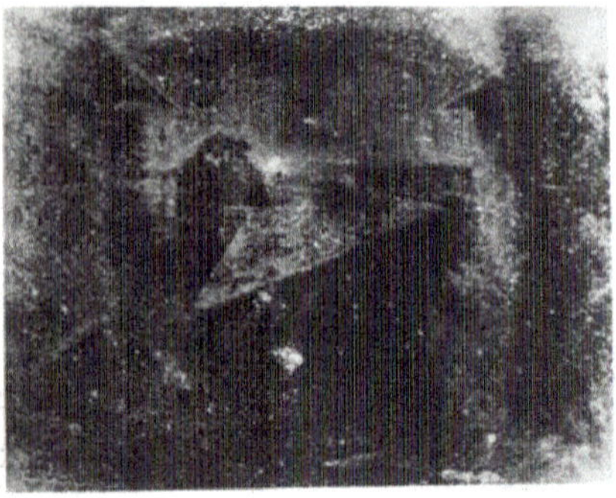

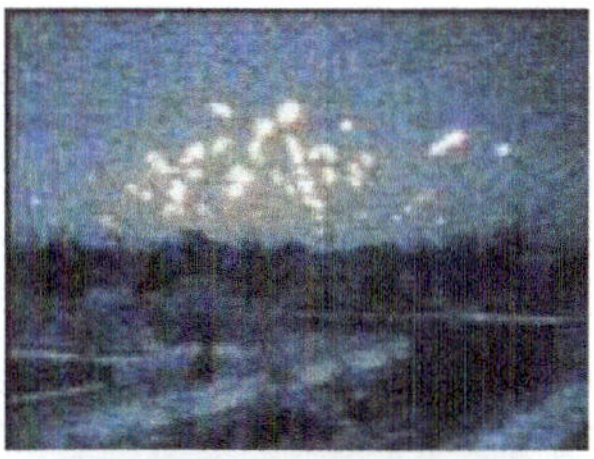

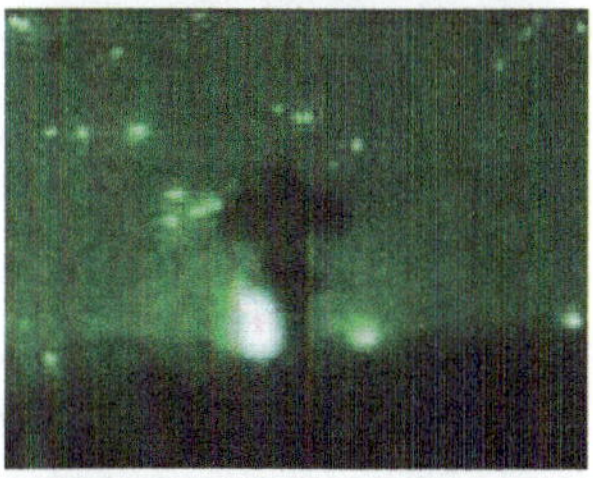

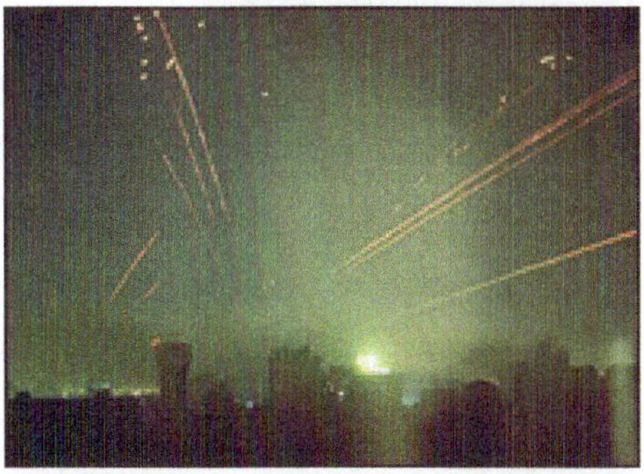

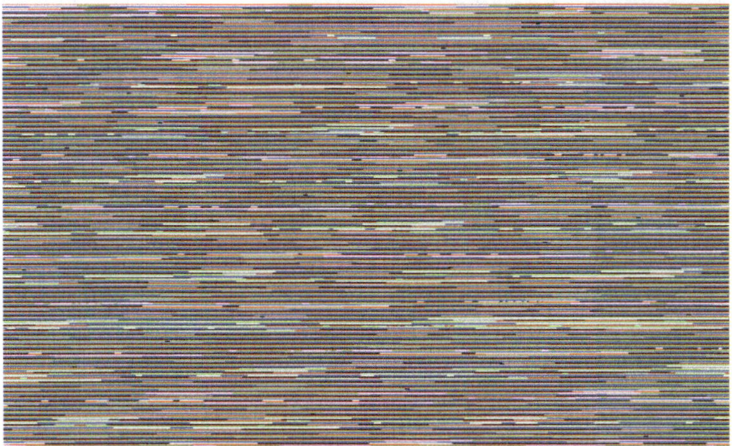

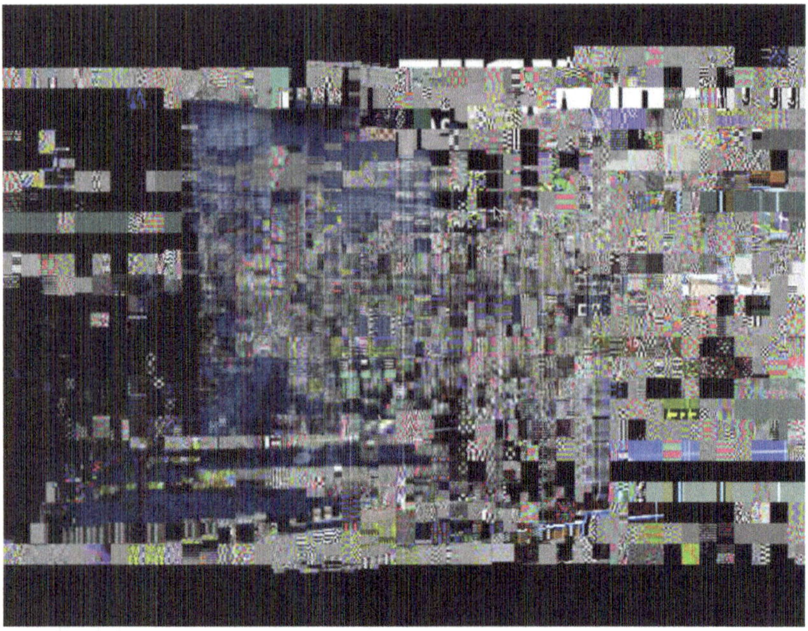

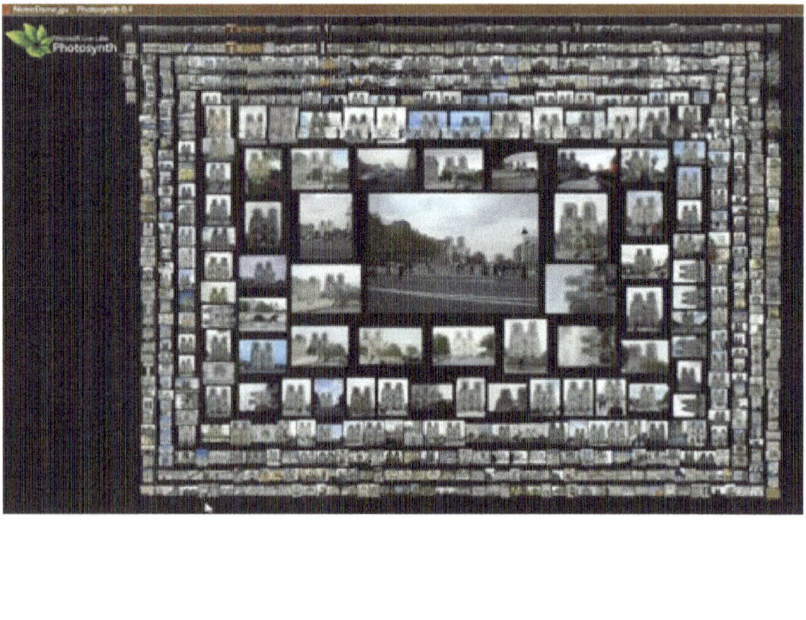
Photosynth

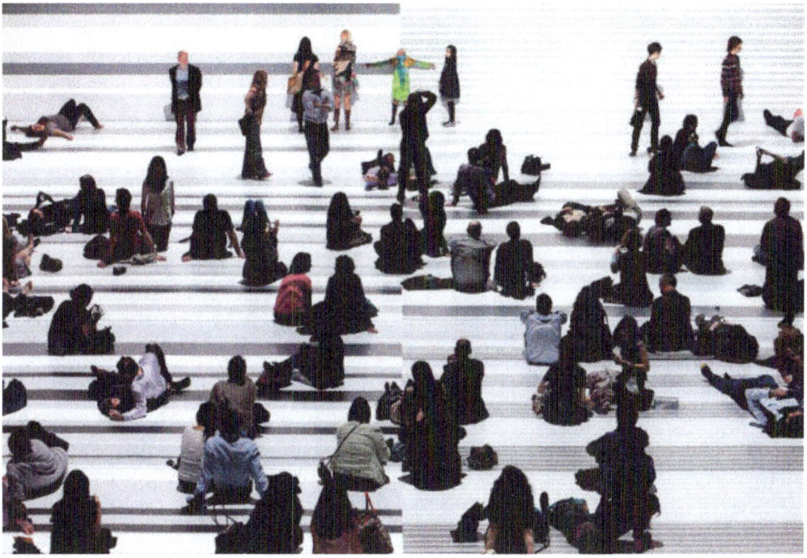

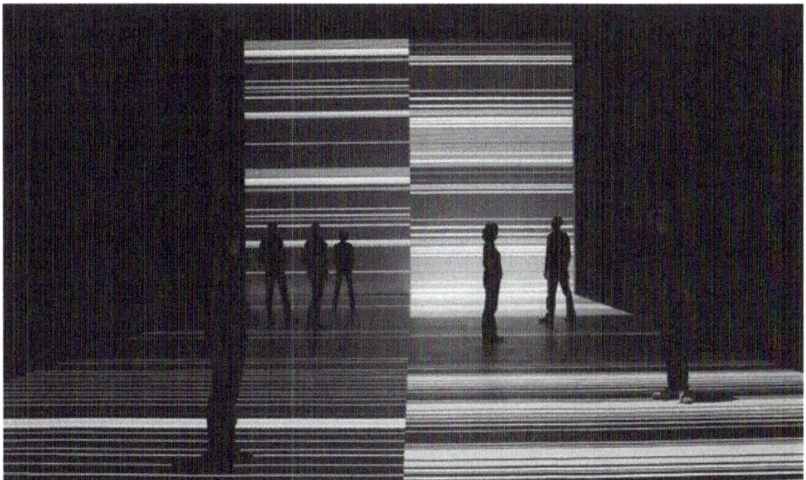

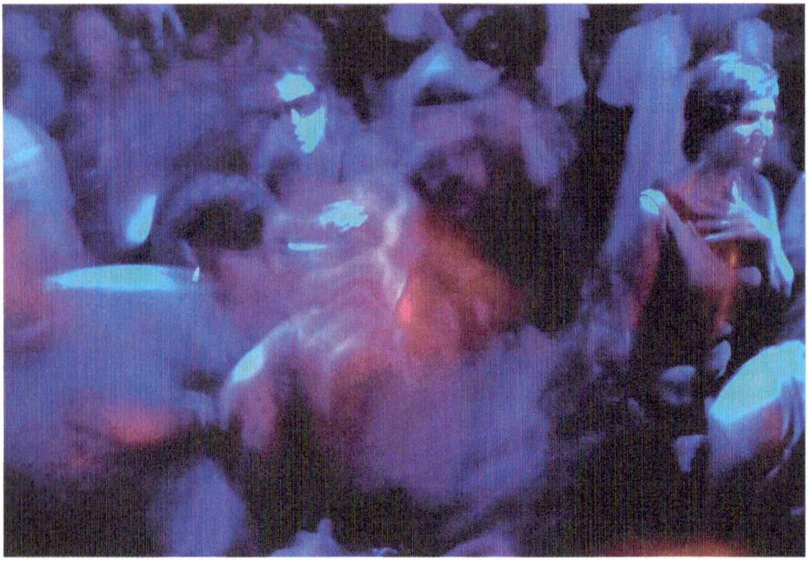

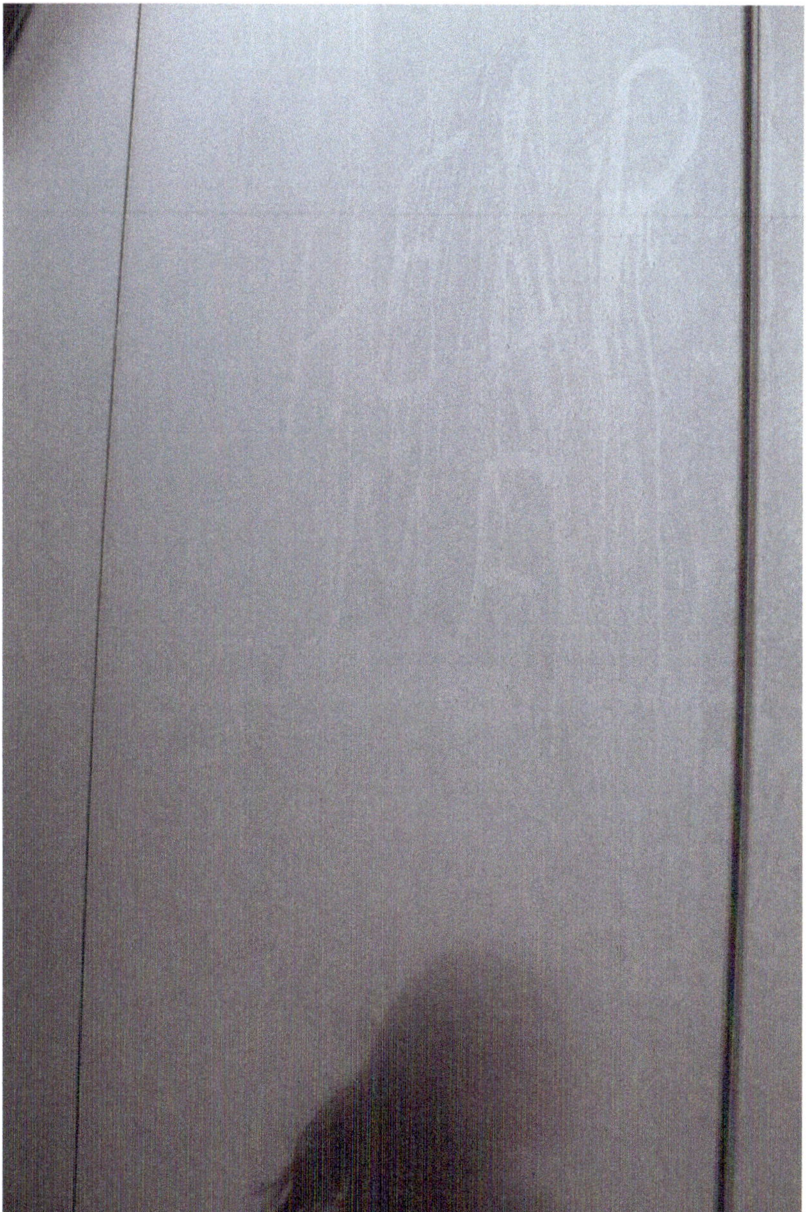

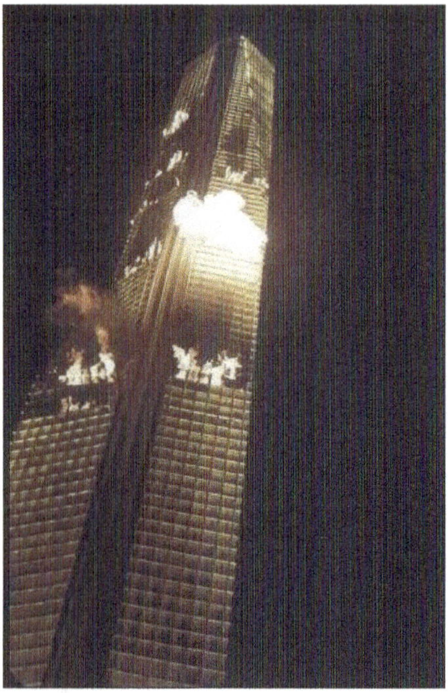

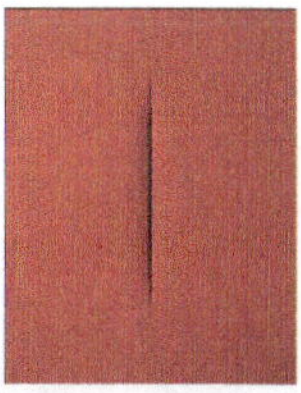

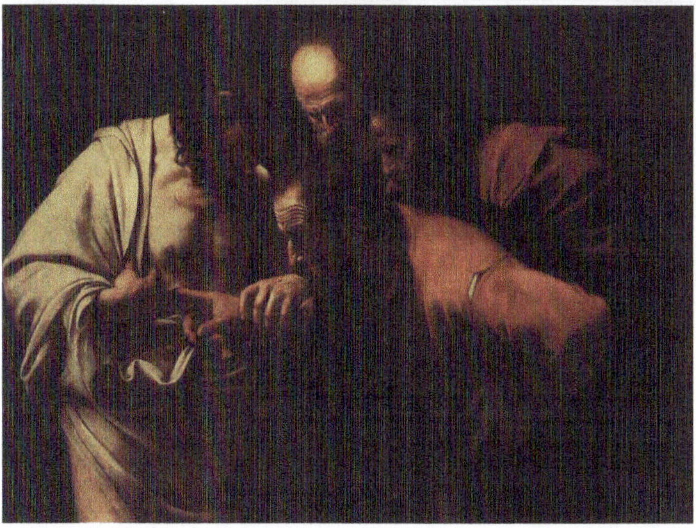

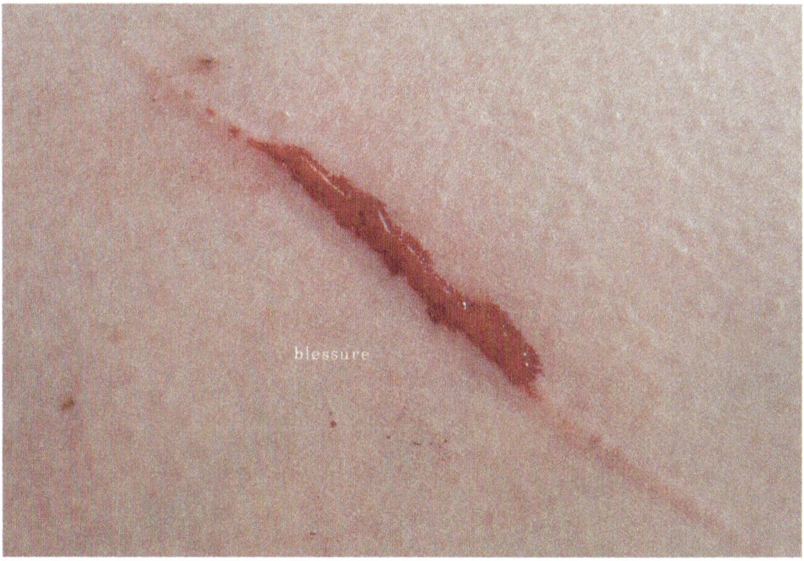
blessure

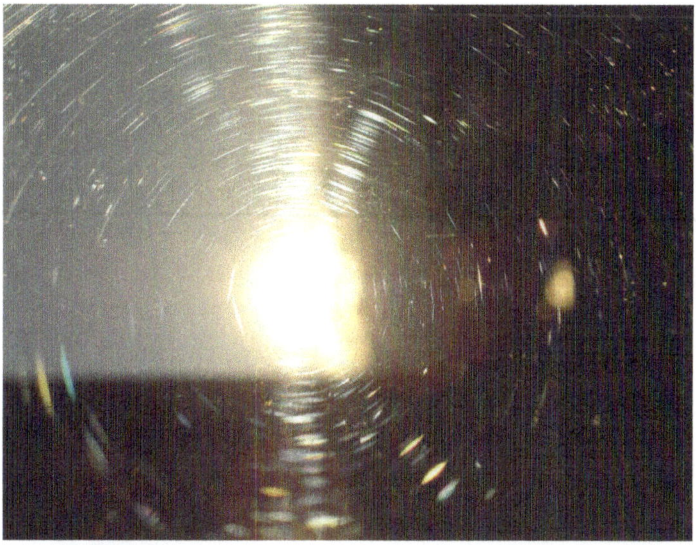

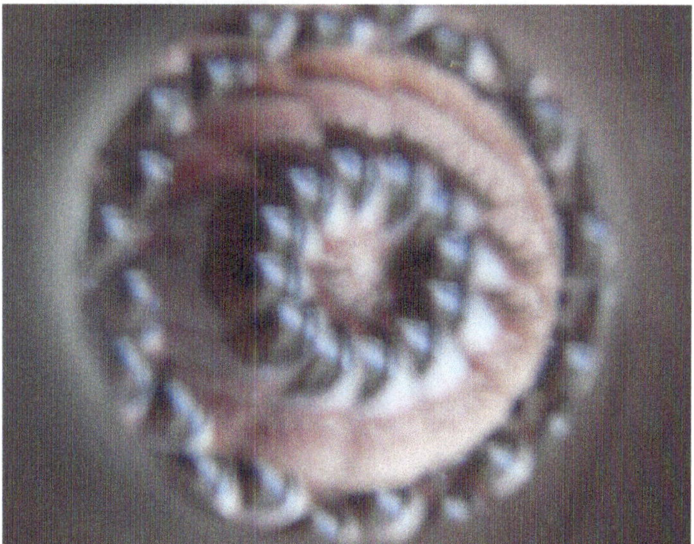

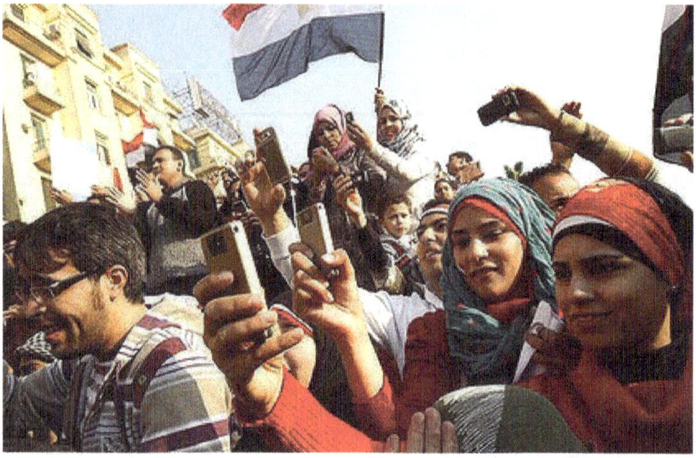

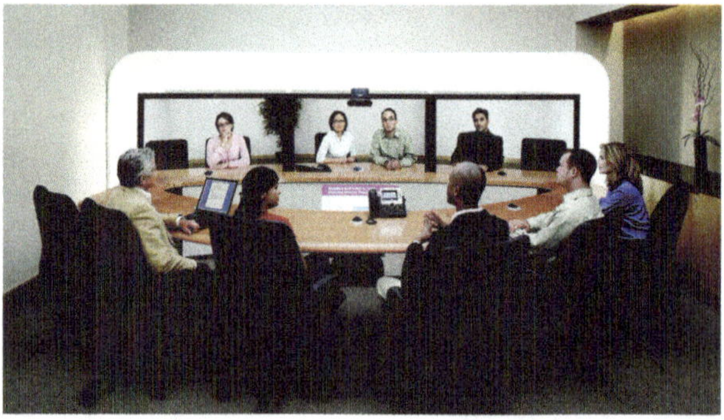

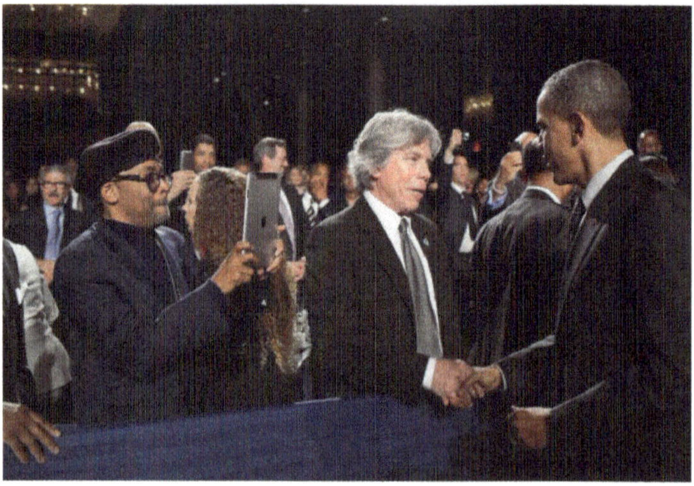

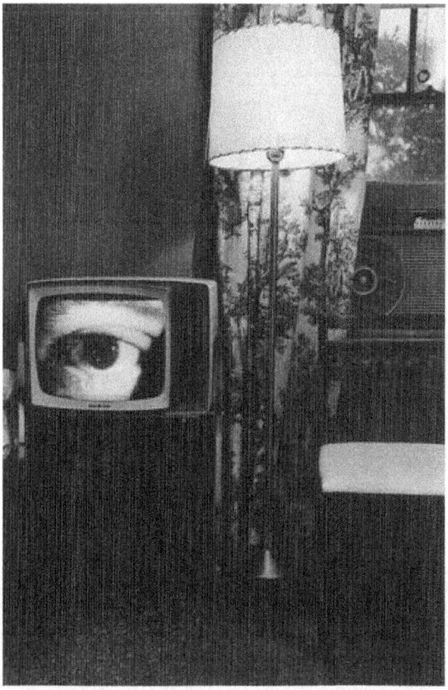

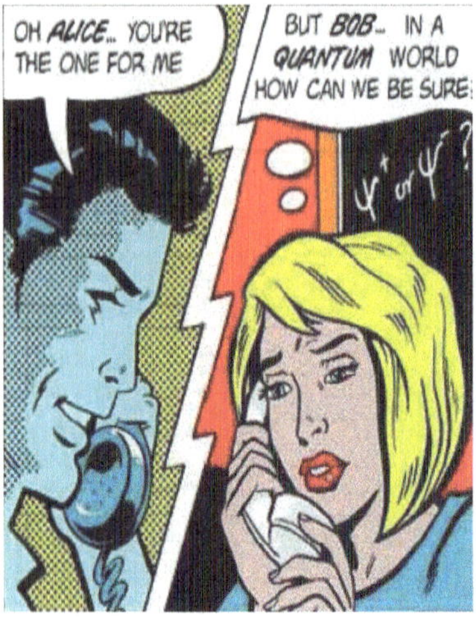
OH ALICE... YOU'RE THE ONE FOR ME
BUT BOB... IN A QUANTUM WORLD HOW CAN WE BE SURE?

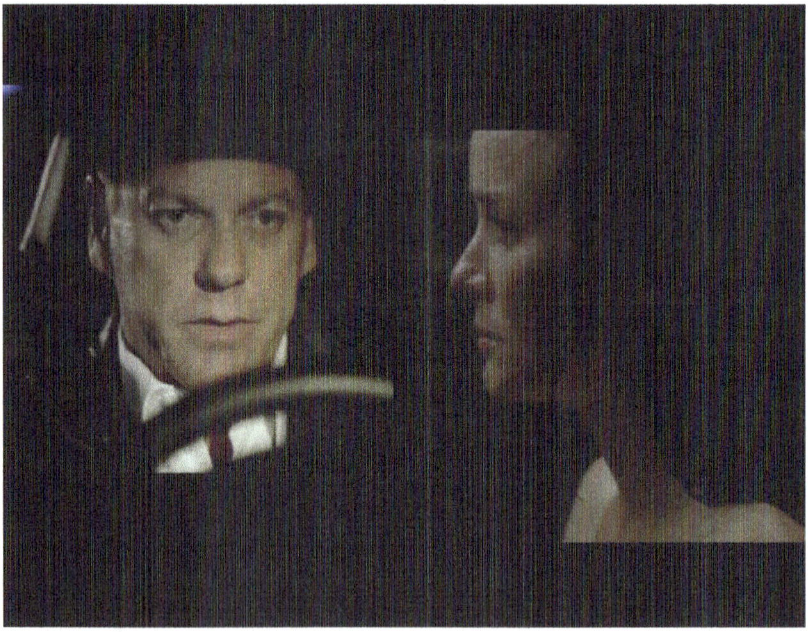

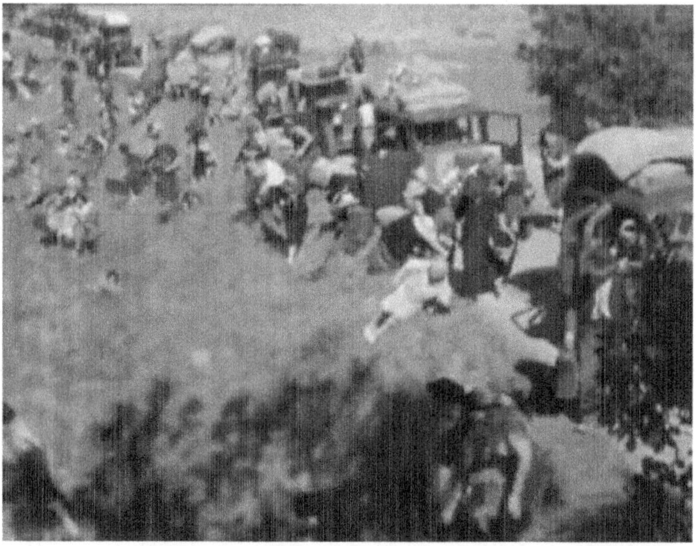

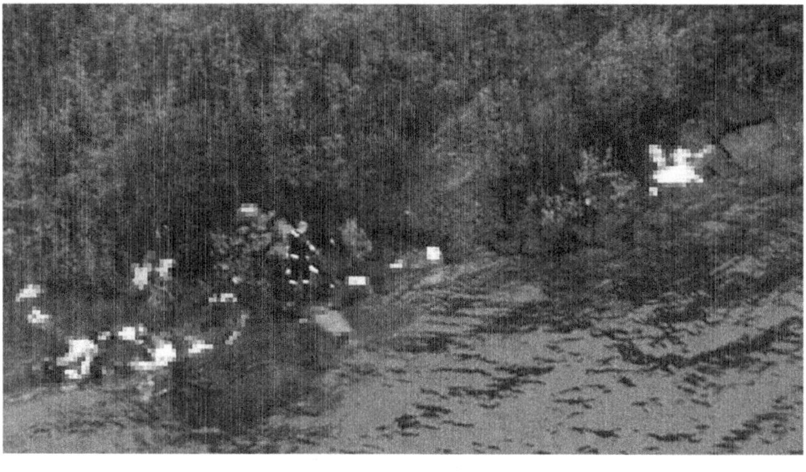

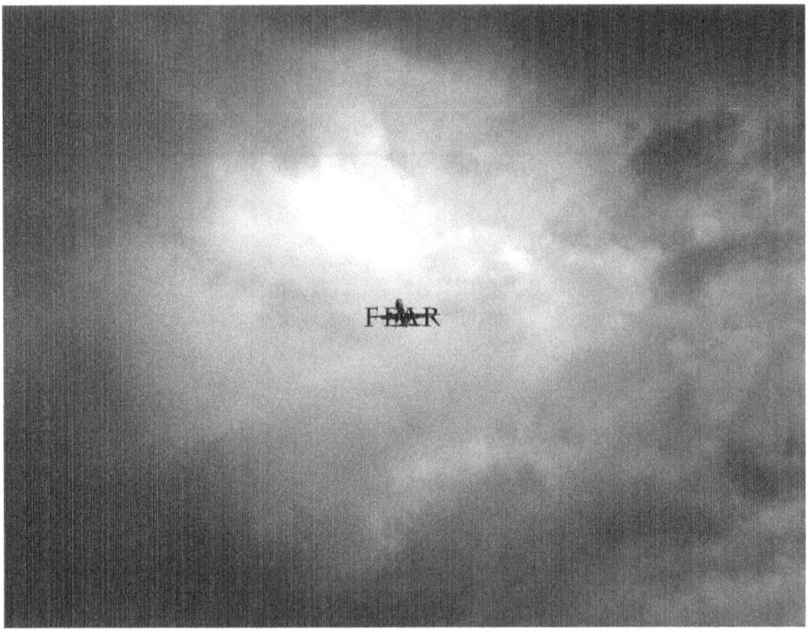
FEAR

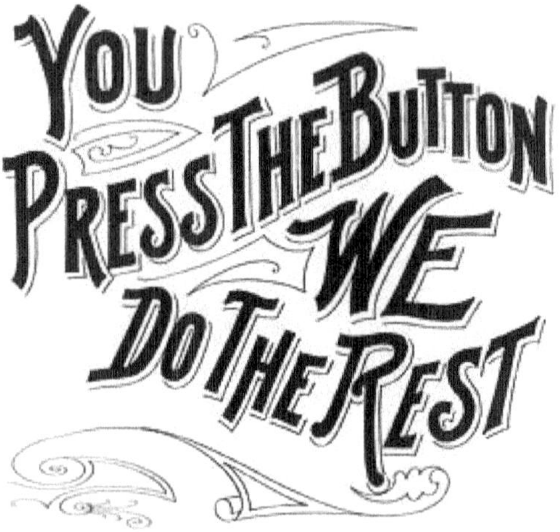
YOU
PRESS THE BUTTON
WE
DO THE REST

Sun, From the series *IMageTeXt*, 2009. (Authors' own work)

Andreas Müller Pohle, *Digital Scores (after Nicéphore Niépce)*, 1995–1998. Here the earliest known photograph is the subject of a series in which analog photography is translated into alphanumeric signs by means of the digital code. "View from his study," taken by Nicéphore Niépce in 1826, required an exposure time of presumably eight hours and could thus never correspond to the human gaze. This photograph was digitized, the information contained in the seven million bytes translated into alphanumeric signs and distributed over eight squares. The panels, unreadable for the human eye, represent the complete binary description of the oldest surviving photograph. The time of representation is thus transformed into the representation of information.

Harry Ransom Center and J. Paul Getty Museum, Color digital print reproduction of Joseph Nicéphore Niépce's *View from the Window at Le Gras* (1826), June 2002.

Kodak Research Laboratory, Harrow, England, Gelatin silver print reproduction of Joseph Nicéphore Niépce's *View from the Window at Le Gras* (1826), March 1952.

Early morning view of the attack on Baghdad from the ninth floor of the Al-Rashid Hotel in the center of Baghdad, 1st Gulf war, January 17th, 1991. (CNN)

Night view of the attack on Baghdad, 1st Gulf war, January 17th, 1991. (CNN)

Anti-aircraft fire lights Baghdad skies as U.S. warplanes strike targets early Jan. 17, 1991, the beginning of the Persian Gulf War. (AP Photo)

Intentionally but randomly corrupted image file, 2008. (Authors' own work)

Corrupted still from the TV series The Wire, 2010. (Authors' own work)

Video still from Blaise Aguera y Arcas demos Photosynth on TED, march 2007, showing the mapping of the cathedral Notre Dame in Paris with images from flickr.

Ryoji Ikeda, *The Transfinite*, The Armory on Park, May 20 – June 11, 2011. Exhibition view of the large-scale digital installation that considers visitors within intangible expressions of digital data and binary code.

Ryoji Ikeda, *The Transfinite*, The Armory on Park, May 20 – June 11, 2011. Exhibition view of the large-scale digital installation that considers visitors within intangible expressions of digital data and binary code.

Untitled, From the fasciae series, Sao Paulo, 2006. (Authors' own work)

Help me, London, 2007. (Authors' own work)

Untitled, Japan, 2008. (Authors' own work)

Film still from the movie *The Towering Inferno*, 1974. (Warner Bros. Pictures)

Lucio Fontana, *Concetto Spaziale, Attesa*, 1965-6.

Caravaggio, *The Incredulity of St. Thomas*, 1601-2. (Sanssouci, Postdam)

Blessure, From the series *IMageTeXt*, 2009. (Authors' own work)

Untitled (Las Vegas at night from the road), 1989. (Authors' own work)

Untitled, From the fasciae series, Geneva, 2010. (Authors' own work)

Experimentation for a series on consciousness, 2008. (Authors' own work)

Tweeting the revolution ... Egyptians use their mobile phone to record celebrations in Cairo's Tahrir Square during last year's Arab Spring uprising, 2011. (AFP)

Cisco TelePresence video conferencing, image taken from online promotion leaflet.

Filmmaker Spike Lee uses his iPad to photograph President Barack Obama as he greets guests at the National Action Network's Keepers of the Dream awards gala in New York, N.Y., April 6, 2011. (Official White House Photo by Pete Souza)

Lee Friedlander, *Washington DC*, 1962.

Alice and Bob, origin of image unknown.

Still from the TV series *24*, season 8, episode 6, 2010. (Fox Networks)

Still from the opening scene of the exodus of June 1940 from the movie *Jeux Interdits* by René Clément, 1952.

Picture taken by a media helicopter of the gunman standing on the shore, surrounded by bodies, Utoya Island Massacre, July 29, 2011.

Fear, From the series *Image TeXt*, 2009. (Author's own work)

Kodak ad, «You press the button we do the rest.», 1888.

Bibliography

Adorno, Theodor. *The Culture Industry: Selected Essays on Mass Culture*. London: Routledge, 2001.

Agamben, Giorgio. *La puissance de la pensée*. Paris: Rivages, 2011.

———. *Qu'est-ce qu'un dispositif?* Paris: Rivages poche, 2007.

———. *Qu'est-ce que le contemporain?* Paris: Rivages poche, 2008.

Amelunxen von, Hubertus, ed. *Photography After Photography: Memory and Representation in the Digital Age*. Munich: Praterinsel, 1995.

Arnheim, Rudolf. *Art and Visual Perception: a Psychology of the Creative Eye*. Rev. and expanded ed. Berkeley: University of California Press, 2004.

Baaquie, Belal E., and François Martin. "Quantum Psyche. Quantum Field Theory of the Human Psyche." *NeuroQuantology* 3, no. 1 (2005): 7–42.

Bakhtin, Mikhail. *Toward a Philosophy of the Act*. Austin: University of Texas Press, 1993.

Banks, William P. *Encyclopedia of Consciousness*. Focal Press, 2009.

Barrouillet, Pierre, Caroline Gauffroy, and Jean-François Lecas. "Mental Models and the Suppositional Account of Conditionals." *Psychological Review* 115, no. 3 (2008): 760–771.

Barthes, Roland. *La chambre claire: note sur la photographie*. Cahiers du cinéma. Paris: Gallimard Seuil, 1980.

Bataille, Georges. *Histoire de l'œil*. Paris: Gallimard, 1993.

Batchen, Geoffrey. *Burning with Desire: The Conception of Photography*. Cambridge, MA: MIT Press, 1997.

———. *Each Wild Idea: Writing, Photography, History*. Cambridge, MA: MIT Press, 2001.

———. "Ectoplasm: Photography in the Digital Age." In *Over Exposed*. New York: New Press, 1999.

———. *Metamorphoses: Photography in the Electronic Age*. New York: Aperture Foundation, 1994.

———. *Photography Degree Zero: Reflections on Roland Barthes's Camera Lucida*. Cambridge, MA: MIT Press, 2009.

Baudrillard, Jean. *Amérique*. Paris: Grasset, 1986.
———. *L'échange impossible*. Paris: Galilée, 1999.
———. *Simulacres et Simulation*. Paris: Galilée, 1981.
Baudry, Yves. "Le dispositif." *Communications* no. 23 (1975): 56–72.
———. "Sémiologie d'une photographie. L'imprévu et le visible." *Communication et langages* no. 111 (1997): 93–101.
Beckett, Samuel. *L'image*. Éditions de Minuit, 1988.
———. *Mal vu mal dit*. Éditions de Minuit, 1981.
Bender, Gretchen, and Timothy Druckrey, eds. *Culture on the Brink: Ideologies of Technology*. Seattle: Bay Press, 1994.
Benjamin, Walter. "A Small History of Photography," 1931.
———. *Illuminations*. Edited by Hannah Arendt. Translated by Harry Zohn. New York: Schocken Books, 1986.
———. *Reflections: Essays, Aphorisms, Autobiographical Writing*. Edited by Demetz Peter. Translated by Jephcott Edmund. New York: Schocken Books, 1986.
———. *Selected Writings Volume 4 1938-1940*. Translated by Edmund Jephcott. Cambridge, MA: The Belknapp Press, 2006.
Berger, John. *Ways of Seeing*. London: Penguin Books, 1972.
Blackmore, Susan. *Consciousness: An Introduction*. Oxford: Oxford University Press, 2004.
Borges, Jorge, and Hurley Andrew. *Collected Stories*. London: Allenlanethe Penguin Press, 2004.
Bronckart, Jean-Paul. *Le projet de Ferdinand de Saussure*. Genève: Droz, 2010.
Buchloh, Benjamin. *Neo-avantgarde and Culture Industry: Essays on European and American Art from 1955 to 1975*. Cambridge, MA: MIT Press, 2003.
Buci-Glucksmann, Christine. *L'œil cartographique de l'art*. Paris: Galilée, 1996.
Buck-Morss, Susan. *The Dialectics of Seeing. Walter Benjamin and the Arcades Project*. Cambridge, MA: MIT Press, 1991.
———. "Visual Studies and Global Imagination." *Papers of Surrealism* no. 2 (summer 2004).
Burgin, Victor. *The Remembered Film*. London: Reaktion, 2004.

———. *Thinking Photography*. London: Macmillan, 1994.

Butler, Judith. *Frames of War: When Is Life Grievable?* London: Verso, 2009.

Cappelletto, Chiara. "Bill Viola ou l'image sans représentation." Edited by Emmanuel de Vienne and Sophie Moiroux. *Images re-vues. Histoire, anthropologie et théorie de l'art* no. 8 (April 20, 2011). http://imagesrevues.revues.org/497.

———. "La natura finzionale dell'immagine nel confronto con le neuroscienze." *PsicoArt – Rivista on Line Di Arte e Psicologia* 1, no. 1 (2010). http://psicoart.unibo.it/article/view/2133.

Castant, Alexandre. *La photographie dans l'œil des passages*. L'art en bref. Paris: L'Harmattan, 2004.

Crary, Jonathan. "Géricault, the Panorama, and Sites of Reality in the Early Nineteenth Century." *Grey Room* no. 9 (Autumn 2002): 5–25.

———. *Suspensions of Perception: Attention, Spectacle, and Modern Culture*. Cambridge, MA: MIT Press, 1999.

———. "Techniques of the Observer." *October* 45 (Summer 1988): 3–35.

———. *Techniques of the Observer: On Vision and Modernity in the Nineteenth Century*. Cambridge, MA: MIT Press, 1990.

———. "Unbinding Vision." *October* 68 (Spring 1994): 21–44.

Crimp, Douglas. "On the Museum's Ruins." *October* 13 (Summer 1980): 41–57.

———. "Pictures." *October* 8 (spring 1979): 75–88.

———. "The Photographic Activity of Postmodernism." *October* 15 (Winter 1980): 91–101.

Debord, Guy. *La société du spectacle*. Paris: Gallimard, 1996.

Debray, Régis. *Vie et mort de l'image: une histoire du regard en occident*. Paris: Gallimard, 1992.

Deleuze, Gilles. *Le pli: Leibniz et le Baroque*. Paris: Éditions de Minuit, 1988.

———. "Leibniz. Le pli, récapitulation. 16.12.1986. Les cours de Gilles Deleuze," December 16, 1986. http://www.webdeleuze.com/php/texte.php?cle=47&groupe=Leibniz&langue=1.

Didi-Huberman, Georges. *Confronting Images: Questioning the Ends*

of a Certain History of Art. Translated by John Goodman. University Park: Pennsylvania State University Press, 2009.
———. *Survivance des lucioles*. Paris: Éditions de Minuit, 2009.
Druckrey, Timothy. "Instability and Dispersion." In *Over Exposed*. New York: New Press, 1999.
Eco, Umberto, Georges Didi-Huberman, and Marc Augé. *L'expérience des images*. INA, 2011.
Elkins, James. *Photography Theory*. New York: Routledge, 2007.
Flusser, Vilém. *Choses et non-choses: Esquisses phénoménologiques*. Nîmes, France: Jacqueline Chambon, 1996.
———. *Into the Universe of Technical Images*. Minneapolis: University of Minnesota Press, 2011.
———. *La civilisation des médias*. Belval, France: Circé, 2006.
———. "On Memory (Electronic or Otherwise)." *Leonardo* 23, no. 4 (1990): 397–399.
———. "On Writing, Complexity and the Technical Revolutions, Interview at the European Media Art Festival, Osnabrück," September 1988. http://www.youtube.com/watch?v=lyfOcAAcoH8.
———. "Television Image and Political Space in the Light of the Romanian Revolution." Kunsthalle, Budapest, 1990. http://www.youtube.com/watch?v=QFTaY2u4NvI.
———. "The City as Wave-Trough in the Image-Flood." Translated by Phil Gochenour. *Critical Inquiry* 31, no. 2 (2005): 320–328.
———. "The Photograph as Post-Industrial Object: An Essay on the Ontological Standing of Photographs." *Leonardo* 19, no. 4 (1986): 329–332.
———. *Towards a Philosophy of Photography*. London: Reaktion, 2000.
———. *Vampyrotheuthis Infernalis*. Translated by Maltez Rodrigo. New York: Atropos Press, n.d.
———. *Writings*. Edited by Andreas Müller-Pohle. 2. Aufl. Minneapolis: University of Minnesota Press, 2005.
Flusser, Vilém. *Essais sur la nature et la culture*. Belval (Vosges): Circé, 2005.

Foster, Hal, ed. *Vision and Visuality*. Discussions in Contemporary Culture 2. Seattle: Bay Press, 1988.

Foucault, Michel. *Dits et écrits, Tome 1: 1954-1975*. Paris: Gallimard, 2001.

———. *Dits et écrits, Tome 2: 1976 - 1988*. Paris: Gallimard, 2001.

———. *L'archéologie du savoir*. Paris: Gallimard, 1994.

———. *Naissance de la clinique*. 8e édition. Paris: Presses Universitaires de France, 2009.

Gauffroy, Caroline, and Pierre Barrouillet. "Heuristic and Analytic Processes in Mental Models for Conditional: An Integrative Developmental Theory." *Developmental Review* no. 29 (2009): 249–282.

Geimer, Peter. "Image as Trace: Speculations About an Undead Paradigm." *Differences* 18, no. 1 (January 1, 2007): 7–28.

Goldberg, Vicki. *Photography in Print: Writings from 1816 to the Present*. Albuquerque: University of New Mexico Press, 1988.

Gross, Charles. "From Imhotep to Rubel and Wiesel The Story of Visual Cortex." In *Cerebral Cortex*. Vol. 12. New York: Plenum Press, 1997.

Heidegger, Martin. *Off the Beaten Track*. Translated by Julian Young and Kenneth Haynes. Cambridge University Press, 2002.

———. *Poetry, Language, Thought*. Translated by Albert Hofstadter. New York: Harper & Row, Publishers, 1975.

———. *Qu'est-ce que la philosophie?* Translated by Kostas Axelos and Jean Beaufret. Paris: Gallimard, 1957.

Hoffman, Donald. *Visual Intelligence: How We Create What We See*. New York: W.W. Norton & Company, 2000.

Holmes, Brian. *Escape the Overcode: Activist Art in the Control Society*. Eindhoven: Van Abbemuseum, 2009.

Holmes, Oliver Wendell. "The Stereoscope and the Stereograph." *The Atlantic*, June 1859. http://www.theatlantic.com/magazine/archive/1859/06/the-stereoscope-and-the-stereograph/3361/.

Jakobson, Roman. "On Realism and Art (1921)." In *Readings in Russian Poetics*. Cambridge, MA: MIT Press, 1971.

Jay, Martin. *Downcast Eyes: The Denigration of Vision in Twentieth-Century French Thought*. Berkeley: University of California Press, 1994.

Jung, Carl Gustav. *Les racines de la conscience*. Paris: Buchet-Chastel, 1971.

———. *Psychologie et alchimie*. Paris: Buchet-Chastel, 2004.

———. *Red Book. Liber Novus*. Edited by Sonu Shamdasani. Translated by Mark Kyvurz, John Peck, and Sonu Shamdasani. Philemon Series & W.W. Norton & Co., 2009.

Kim, Joohan. "Phenomenology of Digital-Being." *Human Studies* no. 24 (2001): 87–111.

Kittler, Friedrich. *Optical Media*. Malden MA: Polity Press, 2009.

Koch, Christof. *The Quest for Consciousness: a Neurobiological Approach*. Denver: Roberts and Co., 2004.

Kracauer, Siegfried. *Das Ornament der Masse*. Frankfurt am Main, 1963.

———. "Die Photographie." *Frankfurter Zeitung* (October 28, 1927): 21–39.

Krauss, Rosalind. "A Note on Photography and the Simulacral." *October* 31 (Winter 1984): 49–68.

———. "Notes on the Index: Seventies Art in America." *October* 3. (Spring 1977): 68–81.

———. *The Optical Unconscious*. Cambridge, MA: MIT Press, 1994.

Ladislav, Matejka, and Krystyna Pomorska, eds. *Readings in Russian Poetics*. Cambridge, MA: MIT Press, 1971.

De Landa, Manuel. *Deleuze: History and Science*. New York: Atropos Press, 2010.

———. *Intensive Science and Virtual Philosophy*. London: Continuum, 2002.

Lindberg, David C. *Theories of Vision from Al-Kindi to Kepler*. Chicago & London: University of Chicago Press, 1981.

Lippard, Lucy. *Six Years: The Dematerialization of the Art Object from 1966 to 1972*. Berkeley: University of California Press, 1997.

Lovink, Geert. *Zero Comments: Blogging and Critical Internet*

Culture. New York: Routledge, 2008.

Lucero-Montano, Alfredo. "On Walter Benjamin's Concept of History." *Philosophos.com*. Accessed August 7, 2011. http://www.philosophos.com/philosophy_article_69.html.

———. "On Walter Benjamin's Historical Materialism." *Astrolabio. Revista internacional de filosofía* no. 10 (2010): 126–131.

Manovich, Lev. *The Language of New Media*. Cambridge, MA: MIT Press, 2002.

———. "The Paradoxes of Digital Photography." In *Photography After Photography*. Munich: Praterinsel, 1996.

Martin, François. "Mécanique quantique et psychisme." Conférence au Département de psychiatrie des Hôpitaux universitaires de Genève le 12 Février 2009.

Martin, François, Federico Carminati, and Giuliana Galli Carminati. "Comments on a Quantum Model of the Psyche," April 2011.

———. "Synchronicity, Quantum Information and the Psyche." *Journal of Cosmology* 3 (2009): 580–589.

Martin, François, and Giuliana Galli Carminati. "Quantum Mechanics and the Psyche." *Physics of Particle and Nuclei* 39, no. 4 (2008): 560–577.

Massumi, Brian. *Parables for the Virtual: Movement, Affect, Sensation*. Post-Contemporary Interventions. Durham & London: Duke University Press Books, 2002.

McLuhan, Marshall. *The Medium is the Massage: An Inventory of Effects*. Corte Madera, CA: Gingko Press, 2001.

Merleau-Ponty, Maurice. *L'œil et l'esprit*. Folio essais. Paris: Gallimard, 1964.

———. *Phenomenology of Perception*. London & New York: Routledge, 2002.

Mitchell, William J. "The Future of the Image: Rancière's Road Not Taken." *Culture, Theory & Critique* no. 50 (2–3) (2009): 133–144.

———. *The Reconfigured Eye. Visual Truth in the Post-photographic Era*. 3rd ed. Cambridge, MA: MIT Press, 1998.

———. "What Is an Image?" *New Literary History* 15, no. 3

(spring 1984): 503–537.
Moholy Nagy, Laszlo. "From Pigment to Light (1936)." In *Photography in Print*. Albuquerque: University of New Mexico Press, 1988.
Nichols, Steve. *The Primal Eye*. steve nichols, 2009.
Noe, Alva. "Is the Visual World a Grand Illusion?" *Journal of Consciousness Studies* 9, no. 5–6 (2002): 1–12.
Parker, John. "The Dialectics of Allegoresis: Historical Materialism in Benjamin's Illuminations." *Other Voices* 1, no. 1 (March 1997). http://www.othervoices.org/1.1/parkerj/benj.php.
Plato. *Timaeus and Critias*. Oxford World's Classics. Oxford: Oxford University Press, 2008.
Polkinghorne, J. *Quantum Theory: a Very Short Introduction*. Oxford & New York: Oxford University Press, 2002.
Pylyshyn, Zenon W. *Seeing and Visualizing: It's Not What You Think*. 1st ed. A Bradford Book, 2006.
———. *Things and Places: How the Mind Connects with the World*. Cambridge, MA: MIT Press, 2011.
Rancière, Jacques. *Le destin des images*. Paris: La Fabrique, 2003.
———. *Le partage du sensible: Esthétique et politique*. Paris: La Fabrique, 2000.
———. *Le spectateur émancipé*. Paris: La Fabrique, 2008.
Rasmussen, Nicolas. *Picture Control: The Electron Microscope and the Transformation of Biology in America, 1940-1960*. New edition. Writing Science. Stanford: Stanford University Press, 1997.
Reinagel, P. "How Do Visual Neurons Respond in the Real World?" *Current Opinion in Neurobiology* 11, no. 4 (August 2001): 437–442.
Ritchin, Fred. *After Photography*. New York: W. W. Norton & Company, 2010.
———. *In our own image: the coming revolution in photography: how computer technology is changing our view of the world*. New York: Aperture, 1990.
Robins, Kevin. *Into the Image: Culture and Politics in the Field of Vision*. London: Routledge, 1996.

Schirmacher, Wolfgang. "Art(ificial) Perception: Nietzsche and Culture After Nihilism." *Poesis* (1999): 4–8.

———. *German 20th Century Philosophical Writings*. Continuum International Publishing Group, 2003.

———. "Homo Generator in Artificial Life: From a Conversation with Jean-François Lyotard." *Poesis 7* (2005): 86–99.

———. "Homo Generator: Media and Postmodern Technology." In *Culture on the Brink: Ideologies of Technology*. Discussions in Contemporary Culture 9, n.d.

———. "Media Aesthetics in Europe." Paris: Association Descartes and College International de Philosophie, 1991. http://www.egs.edu/faculty/wolfgang-schirmacher/articles/media-aesthetics-in-europe/.

———. "Net Culture." *Poesis* 3 (2001).

———. *The essential Schopenhauer : key selections from The world as will and representation and other works*. New York: Harper-Perennial, 2010.

Schroter, Jens. "Archive-Post/photographic." Medien Kunst Netz, 2004. http://www.medienkunstnetz.de/themes/photo_byte/archive_post_photographic/.

Solomon-Godeau, Abigail. *Photography at the Dock: Essays on Photographic History, Institution, and Practices*. Minneapolis: University of Minnesota Press, 1991.

Sontag, Susan. *On Photography*. 1st electronic ed. New York: Rosetta, 2005.

———. *Sur la photographie*. Choix-Essais. Paris: Christian Bourgeois, 1993.

Squiers, Carol. *Over Exposed: Essays on Contemporary Photography*. New York: New Press, 1999.

———. *The Critical Image*. Seattle, WA: Bay Press, 1990.

Stafford, Barbara Maria. *Echo Objects: The Cognitive Work of Images*. Chicago: University of Chicago Press, 2007.

———. *Visual Analogy: Consciousness as the Art of Connecting*. Cambridge, MA: MIT Press, 2001.

Stafford, Barbara, and Frances Terpak. *Devices of Wonder: From the World in a Box to Images on a Screen*. 1st ed.

Los Angeles: Getty Research Institute, 2001.
Sterling, Bruce. *Shaping Things*. Cambridge, MA: MIT Press, 2005.
Stieglitz, Alfred. *Stieglitz on Photography: His Selected Essays and Notes*. 1st ed. New York, NY: Aperture Foundation, 2000.
Szarkowski, John. *The Photographer's Eye*. 1st paperback. New York: The Museum of Modern Art, 1966.
Thagard, Paul. "How Brains Make Mental Models." In *Model-Based Reasoning in Science & Technology*. Berlin Heidelberg: Springer-Verlag, 2010.
Thomas, Nigel J.T. "Visual Imagery and Consciousness." In *Encyclopedia of Consciousness*. Focal Press, 2009.
Tisseron, Serge. "Les pièges de la visibilité." *Les cahiers de médiologies* no. 10 (2000): 188–195.
Tomas, David. "From the Photograph to Postphotographic Practice: Toward a Postoptical Ecology of the Eye." *Substance* no. 55 (1988): 59–68.
Trachtenberg, Alan. *Classic Essays on Photography*. New Haven: Leete's Island Book, 1980.
Tucker, Marcia. *Art After Modernism: Rethinking Representation*. 9th edition. New York: New Museum of Contemporary Art, 1999.
Uexküll, Jakob von. *A foray into the worlds of animals and humans: with A theory of meaning*. Translated by Joseph D. O'Neil. Minneapolis: University of Minnesota Press, 2010.
Virilio, Paul. *Esthétique de la disparition*. Paris: Galilée, 1989.
— — —. *L'art à perte de vue*. Paris: Galilée, 2005.
— — —. *L'université du désastre*. Paris: Galilée, 2007.
— — —. *The Vision Machine*. Bloomington, IN: Indiana University Press, 1994.
Wade, Nicholas J., and Michael T. Swanton. *Visual Perception: An Introduction*. Hove, PA: Psychology Press, 2001.
Wall, Jeff. *Jeff Wall: Essais et entretiens, 1984-2001*. Paris: École nationale supérieure des beaux-arts, 2001.
Walton, Kendall L. "Transparent Pictures: On the Nature of Photographic Realism." *Critical Inquiry* 11, no. 2

(December 1984): 246–277.
Weschler, Lawrence. *Seeing is Forgetting the Name of the Thing One Sees: a Life of Contemporary Artist Robert Irwin*. Berkeley: University of California Press, 1982.
Worringer, Wilhelm. *Abstraction et Einfühlung: Contribution à la psychologie du style*. Paris: Klincksieck, 2003.
Youngblood, Gene. "Cinema and the Code." *Leonardo. Supplemental Issue* 2 (January 1989): 27–30.
Zielinski, Siegfried. *Deep Time of the Media: Toward an Archaeology of Hearing and Seeing by Technical Means*. Cambridge, MA: MIT Press, 2008.
Zielinski, Siegfried, and Eckhard Furlus. *Variantology 3: On Deep Time Relations of Arts, Sciences and Technologies*. Köln: Walther König, 2008.
Zielinski, Siegfried, and David Link. *Variantology 2: On Deep Time Relations of Arts, Sciences and Technologies*. Köln: Walther König, 2006.
Zielinski, Siegfried, and Silvia M. Wagnermaier. *Variantology 1: On Deep Time Relations of Arts, Sciences and Technologies*. Köln: Walther König, 2005.

Think Media: EGS Media Philosophy Series

Wolfgang Schirmacher, *editor*

A Postcognitive Negation: The Sadomasochistic Dialectic of American Psychology, Matthew Giobbi
A World Without Reason, Jeff McGary
All for Nothing, Rachel K. Ward
Asking, for Telling, by Doing, as if Betraying, Stephen David Ross
Memory and Catastrophe, Joan Grossman
Can Computers Create Art?, James Morris
Community without Identity: The Ontology and Politics of Heidegger, Tony See
Deleuze and the Sign, Christopher M. Drohan
Deleuze: History and Science, Manuel DeLanda
DRUGS Rhetoric of Fantasy, Addiction to Truth, Dennis Schep
Facticity, Poverty and Clones: On Kazuo Ishiguro's 'Never Let Me Go', Brian Willems
Fear and Laughter: A Politics of Not Selves 'For' Self, Jake Reeder
Gratitude for Technology, Baruch Gottlieb
Hospitality in the Age of Media Representation, Christian Hänggi
Itself, Robert Craig Baum
Jack Spicer: The Poet as Crystal Radio Set, Matthew Keenan
Laughter and Mourning: point of rupture, Pamela Noensie
Letters to a Young Therapist: Relational Practices for the Coming Community, Vincenzo Di Nicola
Literature as Pure Mediality: Kafka and the Scene of Writing, Paul DeNicola
Media Courage: Impossible Pedagogy in an Artificial Community, Fred Isseks
Metastaesthetics, Nicholas Alexander Hayes
Mirrors triptych technology: Remediation and Translation Figures, Diana Silberman Keller
Necessity of Terrorism political evolution and assimilation, Sharif Abdunnur
No Future Now, Denah Johnston
Nomad X, Drew Minh
On Becoming-Music: Between Boredom and Ecstasy, Peter Price
Painting as Metaphor, Sarah Nind
Performing the Archive: The Transformation of the Archive in Contemporary Art from Repository of Documents to Art Medium, Simone Osthoff
Philosophy of Media Sounds, Michael Schmidt
Polyrhythmic Ethics, Julia Tell
Propaganda of the Dead: Terrorism and Revolution, Mark Reilly
Repetition, Ambivalence and Inarticulateness: Mourning and Memory in Western Heroism, Serena Hashimoto
Resonance: Philosophy for Sonic Art, Peter Price
Schriftzeichen der Wahrheit: Zur Philosophie der Filmsprache, Alexander J. Klemm

Scratch & Sniff, Peter van de Kamp
Shamanism + Cyberspace, Mina Cheon
Sonic Soma: Sound, Body and the Origins of the Alphabet, Elise Kermani
Sovereignty in Singularity: Aporias in Ethics and Aesthetics, Gregory Bray
The Art of the Transpersonal Self: Transformation as Aesthetic and Energetic Practice, Norbert Koppensteiner
The Ethics of Uncertainty: Aporetic Openings, Michael Anker
The Image That Doesn't Want to be Seen, Kenneth Feinstein
The Infinite City: Politics of Speed, Asli Telli Aydemir
The Media Poet, Michelle Cartier
The Novel Imagery: Aesthetic Response as Feral Laboratory, Dawan Stanford
The Organic Organisation: freedom, creativity and the search for fulfilment, Nicholas Ind
The Suicide Bomber; and her gift of death, Jeremy Fernando
The Transreal Political Aesthetics of Crossing Realities, Micha Cárdenas
Theodore, Sofia Fasos
Trans Desire/Affective Cyborgs, Micha Cárdenas
Trans/actions: art, film and death, Bruce Barber
Transience: A poiesis, of dis/appearance, Julia Hölzl
Trauma, Hysteria, Philosophy, Hannes Charen
Upward Crashes Fracture's Topoi: Musil, Kiefer, Darger, Paola Piglia-Veronese

Other books available from Atropos Press

5 Milton Stories (For the Witty, Wise and Worldly Child), Sofia Fasos Korahais
Che Guevara and the Economic Debate in Cuba, Luiz Bernardo Pericás
Grey Ecology, Paul Virilio
heart, speech, this, Gina Rae Foster
Follow Us or Die, Vincent W.J., van Gerven Oei
Just Living: Philosophy in Artificial Life. Collected Works Volume 1, Wolfgang Schirmacher
Laughter, Henri Bergson
Pessoa, The Metaphysical Courier, Judith Balso
Philosophical Essays: from Ancient Creed to Technological Man, Hans Jonas
Philosophy of Culture, Schopenhauer and Tradition, Wolfgang Schirmacher
Talking Cheddo: Teaching Hard Kushitic Truths Liberating PanAfrikanism, Menkowra Manga Clem Marshall
Teletheory, Gregory L. Ulmer
The Tupperware Blitzkrieg, Anthony Metivier
Vilém Flusser's Brazilian Vampyroteuthis Infernalis, Vilém Flusser

CPSIA information can be obtained at www.ICGtesting.com
Printed in the USA
BVOW101419300413

319307BV00001B/1/P

9 780988 517011